D0114156

Blazing the Way

BOOK 3, ACTS 15–28

The
ACTS
of the
HOLY
SPIRIT
Series

BOOK
3

Blazing the Way

A NEW LOOK AT ACTS— SHARING GOD'S POWER THROUGHOUT THE WORLD

C. PETER WAGNER

Regal Books
A Division of Gospel Light
Ventura, California, U.S.A.

Published by Regal Books
A Division of Gospel Light
Ventura, California, U.S.A.
Printed in U.S.A.

Regal Books is a ministry of Gospel Light, an evangelical Christian publisher dedicated to serving the local church. We believe God's vision for Gospel Light is to provide church leaders with biblical, user-friendly materials that will help them evangelize, disciple and minister to children, youth and families.

It is our prayer that this Regal Book will help you discover biblical truth for your own life and help you meet the needs of others. May God richly bless you.

For a free catalog of resources from Regal Books/Gospel Light please contact your Christian supplier or call 1-800-4-GOSPEL.

© Copyright 1995 by C. Peter Wagner
All rights reserved.

All Scripture quotations, unless otherwise indicated, are from *The New King James Version.* Copyright © 1979, 1980, 1982 Thomas Nelson, Inc. Used by permission.

The following Bible versions are also used:
NIV—Scripture quotations are taken from the *Holy Bible, New International Version®. NIV®.* Copyright © 1973, 1978, 1984 by International Bible Society. Used by permission of Zondervan Publishing House. All rights reserved.
TEV—Scripture quotations are from *Today's English Version.* Copyright © American Bible Society 1966, 1971, 1976. Used by permission.

This book is also available in Spanish (ISBN 1-56063-848-6) and Portuguese (1-56063-944-X). Published by Editorial Unilit, Miami, FL.

Library of Congress Cataloging-in-Publication Data
Wagner, C. Peter.
    The Acts of the Holy Spirit series

        Contents: v. 1. Spreading the fire : Acts 1-8—v. 2. Lighting the world : Acts 9-15—v. 3. Blazing the way : Acts 15-28.
        1. Bible. N.T. Acts—Commentaries. I. Title.
BS2625.3.W35 1994
226.6'07—dc20
ISBN 0-8307-1710-2 (v. 1) H.C.
ISBN 0-8307-1718-8 (v. 2) H.C.
ISBN 0-8307-1719-6 (v. 3) H.C.   94-30400

1 2 3 4 5 6 7 8 9 10 11 12 13 14 15 16 17 / 02 01 00 99 98 97 96 95

Rights for publishing this book in other languages are contracted by Gospel Literature International (GLINT). GLINT also provides technical help for the adaptation, translation and publishing of Bible study resources and books in scores of languages worldwide. For further information, contact GLINT, P.O. Box 4060, Ontario, CA 91761-1003, U.S.A., or the publisher.

Contents

"The...disagreement [Paul and Barnabas had] was
overruled for good: instead of one missionary and
pastoral expedition, there were two."

"This chapter...begins with a manifestation of divine
power through the Macedonian vision, and immediately
follows with an extraordinary power encounter with the
Python spirit and a supernatural release from jail during
the first European missionary target—Philippi."

"Paul won in Thessalonica and Berea, but lost in
Athens. He left Athens disappointed, but he had learned
valuable lessons that would help spread the Christian
movement then and now."

"Frontier missionaries such as Paul will not neglect
to care for the believers and the churches they are
responsible for bringing into the Kingdom.
But...some have concluded that Paul's chief priority
must have been Christian nurture....Paul's chief priority never deviated from winning the lost."

"No chapter in Acts could be more helpful for
learning principles of evangelism and more
encouraging regarding potential results for those
willing to move into enemy territory by the power
of the Holy Spirit!"

"In obedience to the Lord, Paul...had no choice but
to move on to Jerusalem and the Jerusalem jail."

"Both Festus and Agrippa agreed that Paul was innocent and that if he had not appealed to Caesar he
could have gone free....It was God's will that Paul go
to Rome, and even if the conditions were not what
he would have wished, he was ready for the trip."

"If all roads led to Rome, then all roads would also
lead out of Rome, and the gospel could, and did,
spread along them."

Introduction to the Acts Series

This commentary on the book of Acts is my first attempt at a verse-by-verse exposition of a book of the Bible. It may be the only one. As a field missionary and a professional missiologist, I have been consumed, more than by any other book, by the Acts of the Apostles, which I regard as a kind of owner's manual for implementing the Great Commission. I have taught Acts for almost 15 years at this writing.

The full rationale for choosing to undertake this massive project is so crucial to understanding Acts as a whole that I began the first book of this series, *Spreading the Fire*, with a whole chapter to explain it.

Because I am not known in the academic world as a biblical scholar, I have asked my friend Professor Russell P. Spittler, who is so known, to peruse the manuscripts prior to publication and to monitor the technical elements of biblical scholarship that appear from time to time. This does not imply Dr. Spittler's personal endorsement of each of my *interpretations* of the biblical text. Many of the themes I discuss fall clearly into areas of contemporary theological dialogue as well as controversy. So many of them do, in fact, that it may be that few readers, if any, will end up agreeing with everything I say!

Be that as it may, I am deeply indebted to Russ Spittler for his wise and knowledgeable counsel, as well as to the several authors of standard commentaries on Acts whom I frequently quote.

C. Peter Wagner
Fuller Theological Seminary
Pasadena, California

....

Introduction to This Book

Some who are reading this book will already have read Book 1 of this three-volume teaching on Acts, *Spreading the Fire* (Acts 1-8). Others will have read Book 2, *Lighting the World* (Acts 9-15). Some may have read both. I imagine that most, whether having read previous volumes or not, will appreciate a brief overview of Acts 1-15 before starting out to explore the rest of Acts. For some, therefore, it will be a review; for others, it will be an introduction to the general approach I am taking in this series.

First, I will explain why I am writing a commentary on the book of Acts; second I will summarize the high points of what I consider notably important through the first 15 chapters of Acts.

Why Another Commentary?

According to a recent computer search, 1,398 commentaries on Acts are currently available. Why, then, commentary number 1,399?

I have been teaching the Acts of the Apostles for almost 15 years, and I have built a substantial personal library of commentaries dealing with this book. The commentaries are excellent and well respected among preachers, teachers and biblical scholars. It has become evident to me, however, that the existing literature contains two general areas of weakness. Let me explain.

Virtually all the commentaries point out that Acts 1:8 serves as an outline of what Luke will be dealing with in the 28 chapters of the book of Acts:

> But you shall receive power when the Holy Spirit
> has come upon you; and you shall be witnesses to Me
> in Jerusalem, and in all Judea and Samaria, and to
> the end of the earth (1:8).

This text, quite plainly, has two emphases: (1) supernatural power, and (2) cross-cultural missions. Interestingly enough, these are the two most evident areas of weakness in the standard commentaries.

By this I do not mean that the classical authors fail to mention these things, but most do so only in passing. Very few have specialized in either of them to any significant degree in their professional ministries, and none whom I have found so far has specialized in both. I, therefore, believe I can make a contribution with commentary number 1,399 because I have been a professional missiologist since 1971, and I have taken a place of leadership both nationally and internationally in areas of power ministries since 1982.

This by no means makes any other commentary obsolete. Each author I am consulting has unique contributions to our total knowledge of the book of Acts, which I regard as a training manual for every Christian. I would not be able to write this commentary without standing on the shoulders of the dedicated and creative scholars who have gone before. I highly recommend several other commentaries, but especially those written by F. F. Bruce, Simon Kistemaker and John Stott. These references, and others, appear in my endnotes.

A phenomenon that seems to lend special urgency to a new commentary of this nature is the veritable explosion of knowledge in the fields of missiology and power ministries over the last two decades or so. As late as 1970, missiology was not recognized as an academic field in the United States. It is now well established. In the 1980s, controversies were raging around the validity of power ministries such as signs and wonders, demonic deliverance and spiritual warfare. In some circles debate continues, but it has cooled down considerably. Prior to 1980, however, supernatural power was hardly a chief topic of discussion among those of us who were not Pentecostals or charismatics. At this writing, however, we are offering five courses on various aspects of power ministries at Fuller Seminary where I teach, and other seminaries are following suit.

It is not surprising, therefore, that our classic commentators of the past would not have dealt with these rapidly expanding areas in the depth it is possible to do today.

Missiological Highlights of Acts 1-15

The book of Acts begins with a group of 120 people from a narrow slice of the demographic pie of the first-century Roman Empire.

For a starter, all the believers were Jews. No Gentiles, or Samaritans—who were half Jewish—were among them. Not only that, the believers were *Hebrew* Jews, residents of Palestine, as opposed to *Hellenistic* Jews who lived in other parts of the Roman Empire. Furthermore, the group was not made up of the more sophisticated *Judean* Hebrew Jews, but rather the backwoods *Galilean* Hebrew Jews from the north, roughly equivalent to what we might describe today as "hillbillies." Not surprisingly, this was the same ethnic group to which Jesus Himself belonged: Aramaic-speaking Galilean Jews.

From Hebrews to Hellenists

This background is important for understanding the missiology of the book of Acts. The first cross-cultural ministry is seen in Acts

2 when, on the Day of Pentecost, large numbers of Hellenistic Jews also became followers of Jesus. As the church grew from 120 to 3,000, then to 15,000 and more, a problem surfaced that is seen sooner or later on virtually every mission field in the world. The church contains two significant people groups—in this case Hebrews and Hellenists—but the leadership is in the hands of only one group here in Jerusalem: the Hebrews. The Hellenists, although possibly a numerical majority by the time of the events in Acts 6, thought they were being discriminated against by the Hebrews, and their widows were not being treated fairly.

The upshot was that the church divided along cultural lines, the apostles remaining in leadership of the Hebrew segment and seven Hellenistic disciples taking the leadership of the Hellenistic segment. I am aware that some may say this is not the usual interpretation of what happened, but *Spreading the Fire* contains substantial material for those who wish to explore it in more depth. Among other things, when the persecution came against the church following Stephen's death, the believers were driven from the city of Jerusalem **except the apostles** (8:1). Many commentators, including me, take this to mean that the *Hellenists* were scattered, but not the *Hebrews*. The division in the church was by then recognized even by the persecutors.

Part of the evangelistic significance of this division reappears in Acts 11: **Now those who were scattered after the persecution that arose over Stephen traveled as far as Phoenicia, Cyprus, and Antioch, preaching the word to no one but the Jews only** (v. 19).

From Jews to Samaritans

A much more radical challenge came very shortly when Philip, who was one of the seven Hellenistic leaders driven from Jerusalem, found himself in the midst of the much-despised

Samaritans. The crucial missiological question then becomes: If Samaritans wish to accept Jesus as their Messiah, do they first have to become Jews? Philip's opinion—and the opinion of Peter and John, who later went to Samaria to check it out—was that they did not have to first become Jews, but rather they could be considered what we might call Messianic Samaritans. This conformed with the brilliant discourse of Stephen, recorded in Acts 7, which offended the unbelieving Jews so much it cost Stephen his life. The missiological importance of this sequence of events is, in my opinion, on a par equal to that of the Council of Jerusalem, which is discussed in the first part of Acts 15, and which I analyzed in detail in *Lighting the World.*

From Jews to Gentiles

From the human standpoint, it would have been virtually impossible for a first-century social scientist, had there been any such thing at that time, to predict that a life-changing religious practice such as accepting Jesus Christ as Savior and Lord could possibly be transferred from Jews to Gentiles. The social and cultural barriers between the two were enormous. Acts 10 and 11, however, records that through extraordinary visions on both sides, God brought together the Jewish apostle Peter with the God-fearing Gentile Cornelius, the result being that Cornelius and his whole household believed and were baptized. Peter, upon returning to Jerusalem, was able to convince the other apostles that such a thing was legitimate.

However, we know of no church being planted as a result of Peter's visit to Cornelius's house. The first church, or churches, characterized as Gentile churches appeared several years later in Antioch of Syria. Ten years prior to this, Hellenistic Jewish believers had been driven out of Jerusalem and some had started Jewish churches in Antioch and elsewhere. But the Gentile churches in Antioch were planted by another group, which I like to call the "Cyprus and Cyrene Mission," because Acts 11 informs us that such was their origin. They specifically targeted the Gentiles in Antioch, and their converts were the first ones ever to be called "Christians."

Paul's conversion is described in Acts 9, but Acts 13 begins to give us the details of the ministry of this great missionary to the Gentiles. For the first time on a massive scale, Gentiles were being invited into the churches and thus into the company of the "people of God" without being circumcised or agreeing to obey the Jewish law. This caused no small commotion when the news reached the leaders of the Jerusalem church, which was still extremely ethnocentric. Some also followed Paul's footsteps and tried to reverse his policies among the Gentile believers. This provoked Paul to write the book of Galatians, and an entire chapter in *Lighting the World* explains the details.

The crucial missiological issue of Gentile circumcision was dealt with on the highest level and had great integrity at the Jerusalem Council, described in Acts 15. The result was an official confirmation of what Paul had already known—namely that Gentiles could be saved and enter God's kingdom without first becoming Jews. This opened the way for the gospel to spread, as it has now done for 2,000 years, to every part of the world.

These are the missiological highlights of *Spreading the Fire* and *Lighting the World*. Now let me mention those highlights relating to power ministries.

Power Ministries in Acts 1-15

It took only 10 days for Jesus' promise of power in Acts 1:8 to materialize. On the Day of Pentecost, the disciples were involved in a miraculous event that was different from anything Jesus

Himself ever did: They shared the gospel in 15 languages they had never learned! Three thousand people were saved as a consequence.

Following **many wonders and signs...done through the apostles** (2:43), Peter and John healed a lame man at the Temple and the number of disciples grew to 5,000 men, conservatively a total of 15,000 persons (see 4:4).

Later, **great fear came upon all the church** (5:11) when God manifested His power in taking life from the hypocrites Ananias and Sapphira (see vv. 1-11). Shortly afterward, so much divine power was released that Peter's shadow itself healed the sick and demons were being cast out. And an angelic visitation released the apostles from prison. Lest we think power ministries were confined to the 12 apostles, Stephen also **did great wonders and signs among the people** (6:8), and multitudes were saved under Philip's ministry upon **hearing and seeing the miracles which he did** (8:6). Neither Stephen nor Philip was among the 12.

A significant power encounter occurred when Simon the Sorcerer, considered by the Samaritans **the great power of God** (8:10), tried to buy supernatural power from the apostles with money. This was a prototype of several incidents of spiritual warfare that are yet to come in our study of Acts. An amazing case of spiritual transport is later recorded when, after he baptized the Ethiopian eunuch, **the Spirit of the Lord caught Philip away, so that the eunuch saw him no more** (v. 39).

The spectacular conversion of the apostle Paul, who previously was Saul the ferocious persecutor of the church, was accompanied with a succession of supernatural manifestations such as a divine visitation in a bright light, a dialogue between Jesus and Paul, a vision, temporary blindness, a prophetic vision for Ananias, healing of Paul's eyesight and a filling of the Holy Spirit (see ch. 9).

Peter reenters the picture by doing power ministries throughout Judea. In Lydda, a people movement begins when Peter heals
Aeneas, who had been paralyzed for eight years (see vv. 33,34),
and at Joppa he raised Dorcas from the dead (see v. 40). Then
God uses prophecies and visions, including Peter's famous vision
of the sheet filled with nonkosher food, to bring together Peter
and Cornelius for the first notable conversion of Gentiles.

The power of intercessory prayer is highlighted by Luke in
Acts 12 where King Herod not only loses his bid to execute
Peter, but also loses his very life. Why? Because **constant prayer
was offered to God for [Peter] by the church** in the home of
Mary, mother of Mark (12:5; see also v. 12).

Paul begins his cross-cultural ministry by participating in a
dramatic power encounter in western Cyprus with a sorcerer, Bar-
Jesus. Paul's successful venture into spiritual warfare brought
about the conversion of the Roman proconsul, Sergius Paulus
(see 13:6-12). In Iconium with Barnabas, the Lord was **granting
signs and wonders to be done by their hands** (14:3). In Lystra,
Paul healed a cripple from birth (see vv. 8-10), and as a part of
the backlash he was stoned to death and subsequently raised from
the dead (see vv. 19,20).

When they finished this term of ministry and were participating in the Council of Jerusalem, the church leaders there **listened
to Barnabas and Paul declaring how many miracles and wonders God had worked through them among the Gentiles**
(15:12).

The implications for the spread of the gospel that these clear
examples of power ministries have for missionary work in our
own day are awesome. I believe we are living in what may well
be the years of the final thrust of world evangelization. Although
some may question such a sweeping statement, I believe I have
evidence to show that virtually everything we read about in the

book of Acts is being reported from many parts of the world today, and the frequency and drama of such tangible manifestations of God's power seem to be increasing almost daily.

We have much more to learn as we pick up Luke's flow of events toward the end of Acts 15.

A Time Line of Acts

Not all scholars agree on the dates for the sequence of events in the book of Acts. Although the matter has been thoroughly researched by competent specialists, consensus has not yet been attained. I do not care to repeat the arguments for different time lines, which are readily accessible in the various critical commentaries, but it is necessary to form an opinion. Here are some of the chief dates and events I am adopting (all dates are A.D.):

30	Pentecost
31	Persecution from fellow Jews becomes severe
32	The gospel moves from the Hebrews to the Jewish Hellenists
	Phillip evangelizes Samaria
	The gospel enters North Africa
33	Saul is converted, travels to Jerusalem
34-36	Paul in Damascus, Arabia, Jerusalem
	Peter evangelizes Judea
37-45	Paul in Cilicia and Syria
	Peter continues in Judea
	The missionaries from Cyprus and Cyrene begin to win Gentiles in Antioch
46	Paul goes to Antioch
	James takes leadership of the Jerusalem church
47-48	Paul's first missionary term
49	Paul's furlough
	The Jerusalem Council
50-52	Paul's second term

52-53	Paul's second furlough
53-57	Paul's third term
57	Paul's furlough and arrest
58-61	Paul in Rome, where he eventually dies
61-62	Paul's possible release (acquittal)
63-64	Paul's final arrest

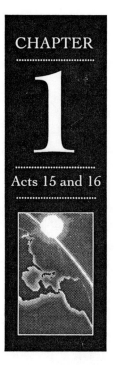

Good-bye, Barnabas; Hello, Silas

Paul and Barnabas had returned from the first episode of cross-cultural, church-planting missionary service ever recorded in Christian history. Fortunately, it was far from the last. For almost 2,000 years since then, hundreds and hundreds of thousands of Christian missionaries have followed their example, moving out to the frontiers where they have searched for and found unreached and unevangelized peoples to share with them the life-giving gospel of Jesus.

These have been men and women called by the Holy Spirit to leave familiar surroundings, to leave families and loved ones, and to leave ambitions for wealth and material prosperity. They have done this so they can be counted among those who are totally dedicated to obey Jesus' command to "Go therefore and make disciples of all the nations, baptizing them in the name of the Father and of the Son and of the Holy Spirit, teaching them to observe all things that I have commanded you" (Matt. 28:19,20).

What Did the Missionaries Learn?

Through the centuries, the people who have participated in the great missionary movements of the Church have differed vastly from one another, but also from Paul and Barnabas. Some have seen great harvests; some have returned with empty arms. Some were short-term; some were career missionaries. Some were married; some were single. They spoke a variety of languages, came from all races, used any available form of transportation and experimented with uncountable varieties of field methodologies. Whatever else they experienced, it could safely be said they all learned important lessons from their missionary experiences.

Paul and Barnabas were no exceptions. Many of the details of what they had learned through planting churches in Cyprus and Galatia would have little direct application for missionaries in other places and at other times. I believe, however, they would likely have seen in retrospect at least three things that have become universal principles for effective missionary work ever since: (1) The real battle for making disciples is a spiritual battle; (2) salvation in Jesus Christ is for *all* individuals in *all* the people groups of the world; and (3) the price for serving God on the front lines is high. Let's look at what this implies for us.

The Real Battle Is a Spiritual Battle

Paul's early warning alert about spiritual warfare came at the time of his conversion on the Damascus road. Appearing to him in person, Jesus had said, among other things, I now send you [to the Gentiles] (Acts 26:17). Not only did Jesus call Paul to be a cross-cultural missionary on the very day of his conversion, but

He also outlined the basic job description. When Paul would arrive among unreached people groups, his task would be **to open their eyes, in order to turn them from darkness to light, and from the power of Satan to God** (v. 18).

Jesus apparently was telling Paul that the unsaved people he would encounter were under a power, namely the power of Satan himself. Paul would later reflect on this when he wrote to the Corinthians that the lost are in fact perishing because "the god of this age" has blinded their minds (see 2 Cor. 4:3,4). Paul's assignment, therefore, was to get the demonic blinders off the minds of the lost and to break Satan's power over them so they could come to God. Jesus was recruiting Paul to join Him in moving toward one of the objectives He had announced in the synagogue in Nazareth, "to proclaim liberty to the captives" (Luke 4:18). Jesus did all this knowing full well that Satan never gives up anyone under his power without a fight. That fight for the salvation of souls is what we know today as "spiritual warfare."

It is significant that when Paul and Barnabas set off on their initial church-planting expedition, the very first anecdote in Luke's account is an unusually dramatic and a high-level episode of spiritual warfare: the power encounter with the sorcerer Bar-Jesus in western Cyprus. Why would I say it was an extraordinarily high-level episode? I explained this in some detail in *Lighting the World*, where I quoted John Stott as saying that in the story Luke "brings before his readers a dramatic power encounter, in which the Holy Spirit overthrew the evil one, the apostle confounded the sorcerer, and the gospel triumphed over the occult."[1]

If Bar-Jesus had been an ordinary sorcerer, Luke might not have so much as mentioned the incident. Such happenings were undoubtedly commonplace in Paul's ministry, as they were in Jesus' ministry. But Bar-Jesus happened to be linked with the highest political authority in the area, the Roman proconsul named Sergius Paulus, and the sorcerer **withstood [the mission-aries], seeking to turn the proconsul away from the faith** (Acts 13:8). The implication was that this encounter would have influence, not just in one person's life or that of a particular family, but of the whole province. The sorcerer was a major obstacle in Paul's assignment **to open their eyes, in order to turn them from darkness to light, and from the power of Satan to God** (26:18).

For one thing, this provoked Paul to refer to Bar-Jesus in such unflattering terms as **"son of the devil," "enemy of all righteousness,"** and **"full of all deceit and all fraud"** (13:10). For another thing, the Holy Spirit chose to manifest His power through Paul by inflicting instant blindness on the sorcerer.

The outcome? **Then the proconsul believed** (v. 12). Luke doesn't choose to mention it, but we can safely presume that many others believed as well.

A Coincidence or Providence?

How significant might it be that this dramatic, high-visibility spiritual battle in Cyprus is the first recorded incident of Paul's overseas missionary career? It seems to me to be much more than a coincidence. If we believe that Luke was writing the book of Acts not only as a historian, but also under the influence of the Holy Spirit who was sovereignly inspiring him to write a historical book that would also become part of the canon of Scripture, divine providence obviously plays a major role.

I have called Acts "God's training manual for every Christian." If this is what Luke and the Holy Spirit had in mind, I would think we could safely regard the power encounter in Cyprus as a paradigm for our own cross-cultural missionary efforts. It is a notice for all who have eyes to see and ears to hear that world evangelization will be essentially a spiritual battle.

That was one of the major things Paul and Barnabas learned during their first term of missionary service.

Lausanne II in Manila

If Paul and Barnabas can point back to at least one occasion through which they learned that the primary battle for world evangelization was spiritual, so can I. This happened during the great international conference in 1989 called "Lausanne II" and held in Manila. At this meeting, 4,500 delegates representing the top evangelical Christian leadership from virtually every nation in the world gathered under the auspices of the Lausanne Committee for World Evangelization to plan strategies for completing Jesus' Great Commission.

Although at this writing it has now become common, Lausanne II has taken its place as the first major Christian consultation group supported 24-hours a day by a team of gifted and experienced intercessors praying on site. At this conference in Manila, I witnessed what I like to refer to as a "living parable."

The evening before the conference was to begin, the intercessors—50 of them from 12 nations—had gathered in the prayer room for personal introductions. Soon after she had introduced herself, a Filipina intercessor, Juana Francisco, suffered a life-threatening attack of asthma. It was so critical that the meeting had to be suspended because of the emergency. In the ensuing chaos, two women who had previously merely been acquainted with each other were suddenly drawn together. One woman, Mary Lance Sisk, was a Presbyterian, and the other woman, Cindy Jacobs, was a postdenominational charismatic. God had revealed to them both that the root cause of Juana Francisco's attack was a Philippine voodoo curse leveled against the whole conference and particularly against the team of intercessors.

Dealing with such curses was not new to either Mary Lance or

Cindy, so they instantly joined hands, invoked the authority that Jesus had given them, and quickly broke the voodoo curse over Juana and the whole meeting. Although a medical doctor present had by then ordered Juana to be hospitalized immediately, once the curse was removed she instantly regained full health.

Reflecting on this incident, the group saw it as a living parable and drew two major lessons from it, among others:

- World evangelization is a life-and-death struggle. Juana Francisco, according to the physician present, easily could have died that evening.
- The spiritual battle for world evangelization will be won or lost to the degree that God's servants hear from Him and are willing to obey what they hear. The women who broke the curse modeled this splendidly on behalf of the whole group.

Whether in Western Cyprus or in Manila, Philippines, or in uncountable other times and places, God continually attempts to impress upon His people that frontline evangelism involves spiritual warfare, at times on very high levels.

Salvation Is for All

The second universal principle of effective missionary work Paul and Barnabas teach us through their first term of service is that salvation in Jesus Christ is for *all* individuals in *all* the people groups of the world.

Actually, before Paul and Barnabas had left Antioch of Syria for Cyprus and Galatia, they had already concluded that Gentiles could indeed be admitted into the church without being circumcised. But I doubt they had any idea of how severe the problem would eventually become once churches composed of largely uncircumcised Gentiles began to multiply so rapidly as a result of their missionary ministry. In Jerusalem, significant numbers of aggressively ethnocentric Jewish believers began launching a campaign against Paul and Barnabas. They went as far as to send so-called Judaizing teams to the churches the missionaries had planted in Galatia, telling them that if Gentiles wanted to be saved, they first must become Jews through circumcision and through agreeing to keep the Jewish law.

This provoked Paul's letter to the Galatians and the subsequent Council of Jerusalem, which officially recognized that Gentiles did not have to be circumcised to be saved.

Among modern missiologists, this principle is called "contextualization." It maintains that cross-cultural missionaries should not attempt to convert the peoples into their own cultural images as part and parcel of the message of the gospel. Although the issue of Gentile circumcision is largely a thing of the past, other issues such as styles of music, plural marriages, relationship to ancestors, church government, theological formulations and many others continue to be hotly discussed in missiological circles today.

And All Are One in Christ

I would be remiss if I were to imply that the Jerusalem Council merely confirmed the intention of God to endorse cultural diversity within the Christian Church. Greeks, Romans and other Gentiles do not have to be deculturalized and transformed into Jews to enjoy His salvation and become full-fledged members of His redeemed people. This was basic.

Actually, the deliberations of the Council—which went on for some days—focused on underlying issues of great complexity. Although agreement was achieved on the issues, the serious questions that initially precipitated convening this meeting did not suddenly evaporate, never to return. Even a casual reading of the New Testament will convey the impression that substantial questions continued to trouble Jewish and Gentile believers alike, long after the Council had faded into history.

After all, Jews had been a distinct people for almost 1,500 years. They knew themselves as the elect people of God—redeemed from Egyptian slavery and commissioned to a lifestyle shaped in every way by God's law. It takes little imagination to realize how they must have prized and guarded their Jewishness. But now they had to accept the fact that in Christ there was neither Jew nor Gentile. God had chosen to unite them with Gentile believers, thereby making them only a small part of the greatly enlarged people of God. We can be sure that from time to time not a few Jews felt that the very heart of their Old Testament Scriptures was somehow abrogated, and set aside.

On the other hand, think of the sense of liberty that came to Gentile Christians. They did not have to be circumcised and become Jews. They did not have to get involved in all the complexities of the law of Moses. They were truly free in Christ to love God and serve Him, with Jesus as their example.

It takes little imagination to see that the new missionary movement launched at Pentecost was in constant danger of polarizing into two separate groups. The Jewish members could easily drift off by themselves, eager to protect their Jewishness. In contrast, the growing number of Gentile members could feel that the Jews were no longer of consequence. God had apparently liberated them from everything Jewish.

In actuality, both Jewish and Gentile believers urgently needed each other—then and now. Both needed deepest agreement regarding the gospel—that it was God's gift through the redemptive death and resurrection of His Son to make people fit for His presence and friendship. To add the dimensions of circumcision and law obedience would have been to question the completeness of Christ's redemptive work. To add human requirements to His sacrifice would be to create a false gospel that would not sat-isfy the holiness and justice of God. If Jewish believers were to drift away from their Gentile counterparts, they would lose sight of the fact that God was saving Gentiles apart from the law. And they would sense little need for the books of the New Testament yet to be written by the apostle Paul, and others, that would explain more fully the grace of God. They would increasingly regard themselves as a mere renewal movement within Jewry, and would draw back from the complicated and demanding task of worldwide evangelism.

On the other hand, if Gentile believers in those early days were to drift away from their Jewish roots, think what this would have done to their faith. The Old Testament would have been increasingly forgotten—its great themes of Creation, the Fall, human depravity, God's sovereignty and holiness, atonement and salvation. They would lose the toughness that would enable the Early Church to stand against pagan corruption—and willingly suffer the consequences, even to martyrdom.

So, then, we should thank God that **it seemed good to the Holy Spirit** (15:28) to lead the apostles and elders in Jerusalem to affirm that there is only one gospel, and it is by grace alone. On this basis, the unity of the Body of Christ was safeguarded, thereby assuring the future dynamic interaction of Jewish and Gentile believers, based on the one Word of God. The mission-ary vehicle the Holy Spirit formed on the Day of Pentecost con-tinued to be multicultural and multiracial. Its members contin-ued to sense the obligation to love and serve one another as they evangelized the nations.

The Price Is High

The third principle emerging from Paul and Barnabas's missionary work is that the price for serving God on the frontlines is often high. This seems to be directly related to the intensity of the spiritual battle. In Revelation, we read that the devil is overcome by the blood of the Lamb, by the word of testimony and by not loving our lives to the death (see 12:11).

Here is a penetrating question for all Christians: Am I willing to give my very life in serving the Lord? Paul and Barnabas had decided that they were prepared to be martyrs for Jesus if they would be so required. In fact, Paul found himself in a worst-case scenario. He was attacked by a mob and actually stoned to death in Lystra. Not a good day for Paul! But God in His mercy brought a group of believers around him who prayed for him and saw God raise him from the dead (see Acts 14:19,20).

Paul later wrote about "stripes above measure," and "in prisons more frequently," and "in deaths often," and being shipwrecked, stoned and robbed. His service to God required weariness, toil, sleeplessness, hunger, thirst, cold and nakedness (see 2 Cor. 11:23-27). Many missionaries today can match Paul almost story for story. The estimate at this writing is that more than 150,000 Christians are giving their lives as martyrs each year. The price clearly is high!

Reorganizing the Mission
Acts 15

After their furlough, Paul and Barnabas were prepared to set out on their second term of missionary service.

> **15:36. Then after some days Paul said to Barnabas, "Let us now go back and visit our brethren in every city where we have preached the word of the Lord, and see how they are doing."**

Paul, by this time firmly recognized as the leader of the mission, decided that it was time to move out once again. The issues of Gentile circumcision had been settled in the Council of Jerusalem, which is explained in detail in *Lighting the World*, and they could now go back and encourage the Gentile churches they had planted on their first term. The most natural thing would be for Paul and Barnabas, who had been through thick and thin together, to maintain their collegiality. But such was not to be, for Barnabas had some unexpected news to break to Paul.

> **37. Now Barnabas was determined to take with them John called Mark.**

Apparently, Paul had previously not been aware of Barnabas's lingering desire to be affiliated with Mark once again. This condition, which for Barnabas had apparently become a nonnegotiable, took Paul by surprise. It caused quite an argument.

> **38. But Paul insisted that they should not take with them the one who had departed from them in Pamphylia, and had not gone with them to the work. 39. Then the contention became so sharp that they parted from one another. And so Barnabas took Mark and sailed to Cyprus.**

I see this event from one perspective as a significant consolation for those of us in missionary work today. If the first missionary agency ever known, headed by such renowned apostolic leadership as Paul and Barnabas, suffered a mission split, we who suffer splits today join a rather distinguished company. I will never forget that in less than a year after Doris and I had arrived in

Bolivia as missionaries, our mission went through a serious split that forced us to move rather quickly from one place to another, much as Barnabas and Mark did. And, like the first missionary split, the fundamental causes were essentially personal differences, although my wife and I happened to be mere spectators, not direct participants in the personality clashes.

Let's pause a bit to analyze what happened to cause the split. As we do, it is good to keep in mind that the Body of Christ in general is characterized by both unity and diversity. Although some people may be disturbed by the proliferation of varieties of churches, denominations, mission agencies and parachurch ministries, I do not share their dismay. By and large, as long as spiritual unity continues to be maintained, the more diversity we enjoy, the more unbelievers we are likely to reach for Christ.

John Mark

Although Mark's name is well known because he later became the author of one of the four Gospels, he is first introduced in Acts because his mother happened to be the hostess for the prayer meeting that saved Peter from being executed by King Herod (see Acts 12:12). Being the son of an intercessor, Mark must have been familiar with prayer and spiritual warfare firsthand. When Paul and Barnabas had delivered the offering from Antioch for the poor in Jerusalem, they invited John Mark to accompany them back to Antioch (see v. 25).

Mark was Barnabas's cousin, according to Colossians 4:10. This by itself could explain much of Barnabas's personal desire to work with him. It obviously would not be an adequate reason, however, for Paul to *refuse* to work with him.

Why would Paul so decisively refuse to allow Mark to rejoin his mission team?

As might be expected, most commentators raise this question, and as Luke does not give us reasons other than that Mark had deserted (see Acts 15:38), it is not surprising that each commentator would offer varying opinions. One commentator says that Mark had a character defect, another that he was not thoroughly dedicated to Christ, another that he unwisely might have reported to the elders in Jerusalem that Paul was allowing uncircumcised Gentiles to join the people of God, and yet another that he was not persevering enough to be a good missionary.

I have an alternate hypothesis, more directly related to the power ministries theme of Acts. Perhaps it was not a coincidence that Mark decided to go home right after the incident of high-level spiritual warfare involving the sorcerer Bar-Jesus in Western Cyprus. Dramatic as the scenario appears in Acts 13, I would not discount the possibility that Luke might have understated it in his account. The episode could well have been similar to many reports my office receives from those doing frontline strategic-level spiritual warfare, describing events with superlatives such as "wild," "intense," "awesome" or "beyond imagination."

Mark's reaction could well have been like that of many today who witness raw confrontation with demonic principalities and powers for the first time. They are terrified by the reality and the blatant wickedness of the forces of darkness. They may believe in theory that demonic forces are at work, but they want nothing to do with them in practice. A good friend of mine who at one time engaged in strategic-level spiritual warfare tried it once at a power point of darkness in a foreign country, immediately fell ill because of a ferocious spiritual backlash, and decided not to do it anymore. Now, he occasionally quarrels with those of us who continue to advocate aggressive confrontation of the forces of evil in the invisible world to prepare the way for effective evangelism.

Paul realized that his future ministry would involve strategic-level spiritual warfare, although he had no way of knowing at that time of his coming encounters with such principalities as the Python spirit in Philippi or Diana of the Ephesians, and undoubtedly many others Luke leaves unrecorded. For Paul to move into enemy territory with a team member who was timid and who questioned the wisdom of Paul's approach, if indeed this describes John Mark, clearly would have been unwise. I would like to suppose that, in calmer moments, Paul and Mark would have agreed mutually that Mark simply was not among those called of God to Paul's particular style of evangelistic ministry.

The Biblical Law of Warfare

If this was the case, and I repeat that it is merely a hypothesis, what I say should not be interpreted as implying that Paul was a member of a kind of spiritual elite—the frontline warriors—while Mark was in some sense lower in God's esteem and a spiritual wimp because he decided to stay home. Elitism in any phase of Christian ministry is a mind-set that must be rejected at all costs, although many of us, me included, have tendencies in unguarded moments to fall into that trap. The best antidote, in my opinion, is a sound, biblical understanding of spiritual gifts. The whole Body cannot and should not be an eye. Paul later writes to the Corinthians, "Those members of the body which we think to be less honorable, on these we bestow greater honor" (1 Cor. 12:23). I have elaborated on these things in detail in my book *Your Spiritual Gifts Can Help Your Church Grow* (Regal Books).

Meanwhile, a quick look at the "law of warfare" in the Old Testament gives us important insight into God's attitude toward those who choose to stay home, rather than go to war. As the Israelites prepared for the war to take the Promised Land, God instructed the men who fell into any one of four categories to stay home: (1) those who had just built a new house; (2) those who had planted a new vineyard; (3) those who were engaged but not yet married; and (4) those who were "fearful and fainthearted" (see Deut. 20:5-8). Might Mark have fit into category number four? If he did, he should not be faulted.

A remarkable thing about Deuteronomy 20 is that it contains no hint that those who stay home for whatever reason are in any way inferior to those who go to war. The same applies to the 31,700 men who went home, leaving Gideon with only 300 men to fight the Midianites (see Judg. 7:1-6). When a similar situation later occurred in David's army, he said, "As his part is who goes down to the battle, so shall his part be who stays by the supplies; they shall share alike" (1 Sam. 30:24).

To conclude the point, Mark subsequently finished well. Years later, when Paul was in the Roman jail toward the end of his career, Mark was with him, according to Colossians 4:10. And when he writes to Timothy, Paul says, "Get Mark and bring him with you, for he is useful to me for ministry" (2 Tim. 4:11). Mark eventually teamed up with Peter, and his mother (who, incidentally, would also be Barnabas's "Aunt Mary") in all likelihood served as Peter's personal intercessor (see Acts 12:5,12). To cap things off, Mark, presumably under Peter's influence, later wrote the Gospel of Mark and thereby gained a permanent position in Christian history.

If Mark was fearful after the Cyprus power encounter, by now he had changed his attitude toward spiritual warfare. Throughout his Gospel, he deals openly with spiritual warfare and power encounter. Among other things, Mark addresses strategic-level spiritual warfare when he records the words of Jesus: "No one can enter a strong man's house and plunder his goods, unless he first binds the strong man. And then he will plunder his house" (Mark 3:27).

Good-bye, Barnabas

Paul and Barnabas had quite a dispute. As Eugene Peterson translates it in *The Message:* "Tempers flared, and they ended up going their separate ways" (Acts 15:39).[2]

What was the problem?

The problem between Paul and Barnabas was significantly different from the problem between Paul and Mark. In neither case are we dealing with a defined *doctrinal* issue as far as we know. In both cases, we are dealing with personalities and the way personal attitudes can translate to behavior in ministry.

An underlying and unresolved issue with Barnabas might well have been Paul's disappointment with him when Barnabas at one point had refused to eat with Gentiles in Antioch. Barnabas's doctrine on Gentile salvation was orthodox enough as shown by his planting, along with Paul, a series of Gentile churches and his subsequent input to the Council of Jerusalem. But when Peter, who had previously eaten with Gentiles, stopped doing so when some Judaizers from the Jerusalem church showed up in Antioch, that was bad enough for Paul. Things became worse when Barnabas joined him, much to the consternation of Paul who forthrightly labeled Barnabas a hypocrite when he wrote the Epistle to the Galatians (see Gal. 2:13). Hypocrites are those who do not practice what they preach, and Paul had interpreted Barnabas's behavior in that light.

Beyond that, their contrasting leadership styles may have been an even greater determining factor in the mission split. Let's look closer at these two personalities.

Barnabas as a Modality Leader

Barnabas stands out as a relational person, fundamentally people oriented. He had a strong need to like people, to be liked by them and to get along well. His name, Barnabas, means "son of encouragement." God used him to encourage fellow believers through generous giving, to encourage Paul when he first went to Jerusalem as a new believer, to encourage uncircumcised

Gentiles, to encourage Peter in Antioch, to encourage the leaders of the Jerusalem church and to encourage his cousin Mark.

No one describes Barnabas better than does D. Edmond Hiebert who calls him "one of the choicest saints of the early Christian church."[3] According to Hiebert, Barnabas "had a gracious personality...he excelled in building bridges of sympathy and understanding across chasms of difference which divided individuals, classes and races...he had a largeness of heart that enabled him to encourage those who failed and to succor the friendless and needy...he did have his faults and shortcomings, but those faults arose out of the very traits that made him such a kind and generous man—his ready sympathy for others' failings and his eagerness to think the best of everyone."[4]

According to this characterization, Barnabas clearly fits the profile of what missiologists today call a "modality leader," as opposed to Paul who would be seen as a "sodality leader." Readers of *Lighting the World* may recall that I explained the difference between modalities and sodalities in some detail when I was analyzing Acts 13. These technical terms, coined by missiologist Ralph D. Winter, relate roughly to what most of us today would call churches (modalities) and parachurch ministries (sodalities).[5]

The modality is essentially a people-oriented structure, designed to serve the people who are a part of it. Peace and harmony are high values. *Being* is seen as superior to *doing*. Process is often more important than goal. Discipline is usually not strictly applied, especially when it might clash with contentment.

Paul as a Sodality Leader

On the other hand, the sodality is task oriented. People are also important in sodalities, but largely to the degree that they contribute to accomplishing the goal of the organization. Discipline is much higher, and people are eligible to be dismissed if they are found to be incompetent and thereby unable (or unwilling) to help accomplish the task. *Being* is important in sodalities, but *doing* is even more important.

According to Ralph Winter, both of these structures play important roles in bringing about God's redemptive purposes in the world. But they should not be confused. Essential differences exist, for example, between First Congregational Church (a modality) and Wycliffe Bible Translators (a sodality). Throughout history, the structure God has used most to extend His kingdom across cultural boundaries into the unreached people groups of the world has been the sodality structure.

This brief explanation of a complex issue makes it easy to see that Barnabas would have been a type of modality leader while Paul would have been a type of sodality leader. Paul cared about people all right, but his personal drive came not so much from ministering to people as from accomplishing his assigned task. Paul said to the Philippians, "One thing I do, forgetting those things which are behind and reaching forward to those things which are ahead, I press toward the goal for the prize of the upward call of God in Christ Jesus" (Phil. 3:13,14). Toward the end of his life, Paul sums up his ministry career: "I have fought the good fight, I have finished the race" (2 Tim. 4:7). At one point, Paul was pragmatic enough to say, "I have become all things to all men, that I might by all means save some" (1 Cor. 9:22).

Now, back to the mission split in Antioch. Paul's consecrated pragmatism surfaces when he obviously seems to care less about hurting the feelings of Mark and Barnabas than he does about being certain in his own mind that his mission team is as highly competent and qualified as possible to accomplish the formidable task just ahead of them.

It is important to recognize that Luke does not describe this mission split as the good guys versus the bad guys. Both are good, and at the end of the day, each will optimally be effective in ministering in areas that best fit the gifts and personalities God has given them. I suppose that about 80 percent of ordained clergy are like Barnabas and essentially people oriented, and only about 20 percent might be task-oriented sodality types like Paul. But, nevertheless, the fact remains that most outreach and mission work gets accomplished by the latter type. This may be one of the reasons Luke never so much as mentions Barnabas again after this volatile incident, although Paul graciously does so in 1 Corinthians 9:6.

I like the way F. F. Bruce optimistically sums it up: "The present disagreement was overruled for good: instead of one missionary and pastoral expedition, there were two."[6]

Hello, Silas

> 15:40. But Paul chose Silas and departed, being commended by the brethren to the grace of God.

Paul now needed to rebuild his mission team. He chose Silas (also called Silvanus) as the replacement for Barnabas. Where Silas was at the time is unclear. He and Judas had previously been sent by the leaders in Jerusalem to bring the report of the Council of Jerusalem to the churches in Antioch, and then we read that **they were sent back with greetings from the brethren to the apostles (v. 33).** Acts 15:34 in *The New King James Version* seems to be confusing, **However, it seemed good to Silas to remain [in Antioch].** A strong scholarly consensus, however, is that this verse was later added to the original manuscript of Acts. So let's assume that Silas had gone back to Jerusalem with Judas and that Paul had called him from there to join his mission.

Why Silas? Why would Silas be a better partner for Paul at this stage of his career than Barnabas? One reason obviously was that Silas did not have a cousin Mark whom he insisted on bringing along. But other than that, I believe another more fundamental difference existed between Silas and Barnabas.

The difference did not lie in their personal characters or statures as mature Christian leaders. Both were recognized as leaders and highly respected by their peers. Both were members of the Jerusalem church, quite possibly charter members. Silas played an important role in the Council of Jerusalem. He is called one of the **leading men among the brethren** (v. 22), which many take to imply that he could have been an elder of the Jerusalem church.

It is not totally clear whether Silas was a Hebrew Jew or a Hellenistic Jew, as was Barnabas. My guess would be that because the Hellenistic believers had been driven out of Jerusalem after the murder of Stephen (see 8:1), leaving only the Hebrew church there, it would be unlikely that one of the elders of the Jerusalem church at that time would have been a Hellenist. If such were the case, it might have been to Paul's advantage to take a Hebrew leader from the Jerusalem church with him when he went back to visit the churches he had planted in Galatia. The Judaizers who had gone and messed up things in the Galatian churches had also come from Jerusalem, and Paul already had anticipated that he would have to engage in some potentially difficult damage control when he arrived. Silas obviously would be an asset. As F. F. Bruce says, "But now, if any one should say, 'But what do they think, or practice, at Jerusalem?' reply could be made: 'Well, here is a leader of the Jerusalem church; he can tell you authoritatively what is thought or done there.'"[7]

A Prophet, Not an Apostle

An even more important difference between Silas and Barnabas, in my opinion, was that Silas was a prophet, not an apostle. Barnabas was an apostle, according to Acts 14:14 (italics added): **When the** *apostles* **Barnabas and Paul heard this.** Subsequent centuries of mission history have revealed that in an active, dynamic mission organization there is ordinarily room for only one leader or apostle. There were not two Hudson Taylors in the China Inland Mission or two Dawson Trotmans in the Navigators or two Cameron Townsends in Wycliffe Bible Translators. It is not surprising, therefore, that Paul and Barnabas, both apostles, would only be able to minister in close contact with each other for a limited time period.

Acts 15:32 (italics added) mentions **Judas and Silas, themselves being *prophets*.** Both apostles, such as Barnabas, and prophets, such as Silas, are essential in the Body of Christ when it is functioning as God designed it. "And He Himself gave some to be apostles, some prophets, some evangelists, and some pastors and teachers" (Eph. 4:11). The gift of apostle is essentially an authority-based gift. Here is my definition:

> The gift of apostle is the special ability that God gives to some members of the Body of Christ to assume and exercise general leadership over a number of churches with an extraordinary authority in spiritual matters that is spontaneously recognized and appreciated by those churches.[8]

Paul, considering his apostolic authority, would welcome a prophet as his colleague. A mutual recognition of spiritual gifts would assure both of them that there would be no questions concerning leadership of the mission as they worked together.*

---

*On the question of Silas's apostleship, some may suppose that Paul refers to him as an apostle in 1 Thessalonians. Paul starts the Epistle with "Paul, Silvanus [Silas], and Timothy" (1:1), and then says later, "Nor did we seek glory from men, either from you or from others, when we might have made demands as apostles of Christ" (2:6). This most probably should be taken as an editorial "we," not a technical designation of Silas as an apostle. Some may disagree.

One additional quality of Silas's that may or may not have been decisive in Paul's choice was that he was, like Paul, a Roman citizen. We learn this when they are later released from the Philippian jail and complain to the authorities, **They have beaten us openly, uncondemned Romans...** (Acts 16:37). When moving from city to city in the first-century Roman Empire, being able to claim citizenship had many advantages.

Avoiding the Syndrome of Church Development

15:41. And he went through Syria and Cilicia, strengthening the churches.

I love Luke's brevity at this point. Paul thought it was necessary to revisit the churches he and Barnabas had planted. He undoubtedly wanted Silas to see firsthand the work they had done and introduce the church leaders in Derbe, Lystra, Iconium and Antioch to Silas. But Paul had no intention of making a career of nurturing these new churches, much as they undoubtedly would have liked him to stay around. By keeping his visits short and moving out to the frontiers as quickly as possible, Paul avoided what some missiologists have called the "syndrome of church development."

The church-development syndrome, annoyingly common in missionary work today, emerges from a confusion of the goals of cross-cultural mission. Usually slowly and subtly, mission agencies begin to twist their priorities. They start with the vision of discipling the nations, but later fall into the trap of placing exaggerated emphasis on developing the new church or churches they have planted. Energies formerly invested in evangelism become diverted into well-intentioned efforts to direct the inner spiritual and organizational growth of the new church. Missionaries originally called to be spiritual "obstetricians" find themselves functioning more and more as spiritual "pediatricians."

There is no question that the baby churches need nurture. The new believers definitely require instruction and pastoral care if they are not to be snatched away by the wolves. But pastoral care should *supplement* evangelism, not *replace* it, as is too often the case. Some missionaries do not realize how much attention they are giving to the 99 sheep that have been found as opposed to moving out to find the one that is lost. George Peters, a missiologist, laments: "The tragedy of the situation is that most evangelical missions are so overloaded with institutionalism that it becomes practically impossible to free personnel for the ministry of evangelism."[9]

Missionaries who follow Paul's excellent model wisely leave the nurturing to those appointed to be pastors and elders of the new churches, while they themselves persist in moving forward to reach the unreached. Thus, like Paul, they avoid the syndrome of church development.

Timothy Signs Up for Warfare
Acts 16

....

16:1. Then he came to Derbe and Lystra.
And behold, a certain disciple was there, named Timothy,
the son of a certain Jewish woman who believed,
but his father was Greek.
2. He was well spoken of by the brethren who
were at Lystra and Iconium.
3. Paul wanted to have him go on with him. And he took

> him and circumcised him because of the Jews who were in
> that region, for they all knew that his father was Greek.

The one thing Luke does stop for in his rapid-fire account of Paul's visits to the new churches is to tell of Timothy joining the mission.

Timothy was a believer, in all probability converted along with his mother when Paul had first evangelized Lystra a couple of years previously. His father was a Gentile, but his mother was a Jew who had raised her child by giving him a thorough knowledge of the Old Testament (see 2 Tim. 3:15). In fact, Timothy's grandmother, Lois, and mother, Eunice, became believers before Timothy did (see 1:5). One of the reasons we think Timothy may have been led to Christ by Paul himself is that several times in his Epistles Paul refers to Timothy as "my son."

During Paul's absence, Timothy apparently had matured as a Christian. **He was well spoken of by the brethren who were at Lystra and Iconium (16:2).** Iconium, as we may recall, was a city about 18 miles or one day's journey from Lystra, so Timothy's reputation had spread beyond the boundaries of his hometown.

The reason I use the subhead "Timothy Signs Up for Warfare" is that his ordination to ministry and to missionary service apparently involved just that. Luke does not give us the details in Acts, but Paul later tells us about it when he writes one of his last Epistles, 1 Timothy. There, he says to Timothy, "Do not neglect the gift that is in you, which was given to you by prophecy with the laying on of the hands of the eldership" (4:14). The city of Lystra at that time would have had several house churches, each one pastored by one or more elders. It is probable that after Paul had invited Timothy to join him and Silas in the mission, some elders of the house churches had met with the missionaries and laid hands on Timothy.

That event, which today some would call an "ordination" or a "commissioning," would presumably have been a meeting characterized, among other things, by much prayer. Not surprisingly, prophecies from God would have been released. Paul could be referring to them when he writes to Timothy: "This charge I commit to you, son Timothy, according to the prophecies previously made concerning you, that by them you may wage the good warfare" (1:18). He also says to Timothy, "Fight the good fight" (6:12); and "You therefore must endure hardship as a good soldier of Jesus Christ" (2 Tim. 2:3); and "No one engaged in warfare entangles himself with the affairs of this life, that he may please him who enlisted him as a soldier" (v. 4). Such consistent military language hints strongly that when Timothy signed up for Paul's mission, he signed up for warfare.

Why Was Timothy Circumcised?

Paul was known as the apostle to the uncircumcision. In his Epistle to the Galatians and in the Council of Jerusalem, he strongly argued that circumcision was not necessary for salvation, and his viewpoint was accepted and has continued to be accepted by the Christian Church ever since. That is why it at first seems strange that Paul took Timothy **and circumcised him because of the Jews who were in that region** (Acts 16:3).

Obviously, Paul circumcised Timothy not because it would have been necessary for his salvation. He had been saved for two years before he was circumcised. The reason for circumcision was not *theological*; it was *missiological*. If Timothy had simply stayed there in Lystra, he probably never would have been circumcised. Furthermore, if he had not been half Jewish there would be no reason for him to be circumcised. He, in that case, would have been like the Gentile Titus of whom Paul says, "Yet not even Titus who was with me, being a Greek, was compelled to be circumcised" (Gal. 2:3).

But because Paul's modus operandi was to reside in the Jewish quarters in the unreached cities he was evangelizing and to attend the synagogues, he had to flex in whatever way was necessary to avoid offending the Jews who lived there. Again, Paul's characteristic pragmatism came into play. As he said of himself, "to the Jews I became as a Jew, that I might win Jews; to those who are under the law, as under the law, that I might win those who are under the law" (1 Cor. 9:20). To use modern missiological language, Paul was "contextualizing" his behavior. His strategy was "seeker sensitive." He said, "I have become all things to all men, that I might by all means save some" (v. 22).

In Paul's future mission, the most receptive people awaiting him would be found in the synagogue communities. Only if Timothy were circumcised would he be admitted, along with Paul and Silas, into the synagogues and into the houses of the Jews. This social relationship was absolutely essential for the effective functioning of Paul's approach to evangelizing the cities to which God had called him. By circumcising Timothy, Paul was not violating any doctrinal principle, nor was he ashamed of the gospel. As a good missionary, he was wise enough and flexible enough to remove beforehand any possible social or cultural obstacle to the gospel of the Kingdom.

The Jeruʃalem Decreeʃ

16:4. And as they went through the cities, they delivered to them the decrees to keep, which were determined by the apostles and elders at Jerusalem.

The only other thing Luke chooses to mention about the visit to the new churches in Galatia concerns the decrees that came out of the Council of Jerusalem. Let's refresh our memories:

> **15:28. For it seemed good to the Holy Spirit,**
> **and to us, to lay upon you no greater burden**
> **than these necessary things:**
> **29. that you abstain from**
> **things offered to idols, from blood, from things**
> **strangled, and from sexual immorality.**

When it comes right down to it, the Jerusalem Council was not primarily about idolatry or blood sausage or extramarital affairs. It was about whether Gentiles first had to become Jews to be saved. And the major symbol of the issue was circumcision. The Council boldly decided that Gentiles could become part of God's people, the Body of Christ, without becoming Jews or being circumcised. These "Jerusalem decrees" seem to be more in the nature of an amendment to the main motion by some who might have leaned in the opposite direction and who wanted to salvage the situation and keep the Council from possibly being viewed as anti-Semitic. In a conciliatory spirit, the Council thereby agreed to include some issues dealt with in the Jewish law in the letter they would send out to the churches.

Notice that the decrees were sent only to a limited number of churches, namely those in **Antioch, Syria, and Cilicia** (v. 23). Judas and Silas were sent to deliver them to Antioch, and Paul and Silas were later to deliver them to the churches in Galatia (Cilicia). After this, we hear no more of the decrees. When Paul deals at length with the matter of eating meat offered to idols in 1 Corinthians, he does not so much as mention the Jerusalem decrees he had previously delivered to the Galatian churches, although abstaining from meat offered to idols was one of the prescribed items.

The Churches Multiplied

16:5. So the churches were strengthened in the faith, and increased in number daily.

Here is another of Luke's characteristic church-growth reports. Even when Paul was not explicitly evangelizing, Luke is eager to indicate that his ministry helped multiply churches. Part of Paul's influence in the new churches was, undoubtedly, to stir them to evangelize the lost in their cities and to plant new house churches in every neighborhood. No missiological principle is more important than saturation church planting, and Paul was doing his best to help make it happen. God had used Paul to light the fire, and then sent him back to blaze the way.

God's kingdom was continuing to advance.

Reflection Questions

1. Think about the fact that all missionaries have experiences different from that of other missionaries. Name four or five missionaries whose ministries you respect, and describe their differing experiences.
2. Evangelizing the lost is a multifaceted undertaking. Do you agree that the *primary* facet is a spiritual battle? Explain your opinion.
3. Do you agree with the suggestion that John Mark may have returned home after the power encounter with Bar-Jesus on Cyprus because he did not feel called to high-level spiritual warfare? Why or why not?

4. See if you can define "modalities" and "sodalities" in your own words. In this context, would you personally identify more closely with Barnabas or with Paul?
5. Why should evangelistic missions try to avoid the "syndrome of church development"? Can you think of any missions today that honestly have avoided it?

Notes

1. John Stott, *The Spirit, the Church, and the World: The Message of Acts* (Downers Grove, Ill.: InterVarsity Press, 1990), p. 220.
2. Eugene H. Peterson, *The Message: The New Testament in Contemporary English* (Colorado Springs: NavPress, 1994), p. 323.
3. D. Edmond Hiebert, *Personalities Around Paul* (Chicago: Moody Press, 1973), p. 62.
4. Ibid.
5. For those who would like more information about modality-sodality theory, I recommend Ralph D. Winter's groundbreaking essay "The Two Structures of God's Redemptive Mission," *Missiology: An International Review* (January 1974): 121-139; and the chapter "Why Bill Bright Is Not Your Pastor" in my book *Leading Your Church to Growth* (Ventura, Calif.: Regal Books, 1984), pp. 141-166.
6. F. F. Bruce, *The Book of Acts* (Grand Rapids: William B. Eerdmans Publishing Company, 1988), p. 302.
7. F. F. Bruce, *The Pauline Circle* (Grand Rapids: William B. Eerdmans Publishing Company, 1985), pp. 25-26.
8. C. Peter Wagner, *Your Spiritual Gifts Can Help Your Church Grow* (Ventura, Calif.: Regal Books, 1979; revised edition, 1994), pp. 181-182.
9. George W. Peters, "An Analysis from Africa," *Africa Pulse*, no. 2 (March 1970): 2.

CHAPTER

2

Acts 16

To Europe
with Power

Did you ever have the experience of sensing that the Lord was leading you to do something really significant, even to the point of telling others about your decision, and then finding out you were wrong? For many of us, me included, the question is not whether such a thing has ever happened, but, rather, how many times it might have happened!

One of the things I like best about Acts is that Luke, the author, is not inhibited about telling the story of the ministry of the apostles just like it was. I love it because it is a consolation to know that the great heroes of the faith in the first century were as capable of blowing it from time to time as we are today. If the apostle Paul were perfect, I would have a difficult time identifying with him. But because he obviously wasn't perfect, I can say that if Paul, considering all his shortcomings, could be a faithful servant of God, there is no reason why I can't, or why my students can't, or why my colleagues can't.

In the following case, Paul went through one of those experiences of missing what God was trying to say to him. Not just once, but twice!

Two False Starts

16:6. Now when they had gone through Phrygia and the region of Galatia, they were forbidden by the Holy Spirit to preach the word in Asia.
7. After they had come to Mysia, they tried to go into Bithynia, but the Spirit did not permit them.

As we saw in the last chapter, Luke's way of relating the missionaries' visits to the churches they had planted is to do it relatively rapidly. The syndrome of church development was not allowed to establish a foothold. As they finished ministering to the churches in Galatia, Paul, Silas and Timothy then set out, as good frontier missionaries should, to reach more unreached peoples with the gospel. Their problem was that this time they went the wrong way!

It is safe to assume that Paul and his fellow missionaries did not set out for Asia haphazardly. That was not Paul's ordinary way of doing things. Much thought and much prayer must have gone into the decision to plant churches in Asia. Ernst Haenchen suggests, quite plausibly, that as far as Paul's human reasoning would be concerned, he had learned from experience that his primary evangelistic target would be the synagogue community in the Jewish quarters of the larger Greek-speaking cities. Haenchen says, "With all his obedience to the will of God [Paul] yet did not neglect at each point to consider the situation exactly."[1] In this case, Asia Minor and the city of Ephesus would be a natural.

Not only would good missionary strategy affirm that Ephesus was a strategic target, but we cannot discount the fact that the missionaries would also have spent much time in sincere prayer. They would have been seeking God's specific leading, which they must have concluded was Asia. Picking up on what I have stressed several times throughout this series on Acts, God's servants in the first century would frequently have answered the question "Why are you doing what you are doing?" by responding with words to the effect: "Because God told me to." In most cases, this would be an accurate response. It certainly would have been, for example, when Paul and Barnabas left Antioch of Syria for their first term of missionary service, because **the Holy Spirit [had] said, "Now separate to Me Barnabas and Saul for the work to which I have called them"** (13:2). Many other examples could be cited.

Missing God's Will

I am a strong advocate of hearing from God and acting on what we hear today, just as it was done in the first century. But I am also aware that if this procedure is misused, it can become presumption rather than providence. This story about Paul helps us take a more balanced view. Suppose that, on the night before they left Lystra, someone would have asked the missionaries, "Why are you heading for Asia?" We, of course, do not know if Paul would have replied, "Because God told us to," but if he had, he would have been wrong. I would rather imagine that Paul might have said what we ourselves should say in most similar situations: "We sense that this is the direction God wants us to go." If it later becomes evident that we missed God's will this time, we do not then need to attempt to explain why God might have said the wrong thing. We simply have to humble ourselves and admit that we sensed God's leading inaccurately. Missing God's will, then, is seen as *our* fault, not God's!

By what means **they were forbidden by the Holy Spirit to**

preach the word in Asia (16:6) we do not know. From the way Luke says it, however, we could safely assume that if someone had asked Paul, "Why are you turning around?" he, in this case *accurately*, could well have replied, "Because God told us to."

It is important to understand that our well-laid plans are sometimes changed by the Holy Spirit, as in this case, but that at other times they can equally be obstructed by the devil. Paul makes this clear when he later writes a letter to the church he would plant in Thessalonica, and says, "Therefore we wanted to come to you—even I, Paul, time and again—but Satan hindered us" (1 Thess. 2:18). Only by intimacy with the Father in prayer and maintaining the fullness of the Holy Spirit in our daily lives will we be able accurately to discern whether we should turn around and go back because God wants us to, or whether we should courageously push on ahead because the obstacle has been placed in our way by the enemy.

Paul, Silas and Timothy went back, in this case to Mysia. Who knows if they might have found the first-century equivalent of a condominium on the shores of the Bosphorus to rest and recuperate from their setback. If they did, I could imagine they would have held a field-council meeting in Mysia and drawn up a new set of detailed plans about why they should now set out to evangelize Bithynia. According to the criteria on which they might have previously chosen Ephesus, the Greek cities of Nicaea and Nicomedia would have been logical targets for church planting. There, they would find many "unreached peoples" in the true sense of the phrase. So **they tried to go into Bithynia, but the Spirit did not permit them** (Acts 16:7). Two strikes on the missionaries!

What now?

8. So passing by Mysia, they came down to Troas.

This time they could well have been too upset to stop and rest in Mysia as they had done previously. The missionaries headed to Troas. But why there? Ernst Haenchen offers an interesting suggestion. If they were operating on the same assumptions we think might have pointed them first toward Asia and then toward Bithynia, they could now have targeted Greek cities in Greece itself. As Haenchen says, heading for Troas "does not yet mean that Paul now set out for Macedonia—he could have waited for a ship which would bring him and his companions directly to Greece."[2] If that is the case, poor Paul was up against a "three strikes and you're out" situation. It was time for God to step in more directly and be sure the missionaries were headed in the right direction.

The Macedonian Vision

9. And a vision appeared to Paul in the night. A man of Macedonia stood and pleaded with him, saying, "Come over to Macedonia and help us."
10. Now after he had seen the vision, immediately we sought to go to Macedonia, concluding that the Lord had called us to preach the gospel to them.

God's initiative for directing the missionaries was now decisive. The indirect way didn't seem to work in this case, so a more tangible approach was in order. God gave Paul a night vision. It is interesting how matter-of-factly Luke mentions that Paul had a vision. Those who have a first-century pre-Enlightenment worldview such as Paul had, would not consider it unusual for supernatural beings—those of darkness as well as those of light—to communicate with human beings through visions and dreams. For example, Paul's conversion experience on the road to

Damascus also included a vision in which he actually saw Jesus, as I explained in *Lighting the World*. Visions were such an assumed part of common life that there is no telling how many other visions Paul might have had between his conversion some 16 years previously and now. Luke would have had no particular reason to mention them.

But Luke does mention this particular vision because through it God was directing the penetration of the gospel for the very first time into Europe. I call this chapter "To Europe with Power" because it begins with a manifestation of divine power through the Macedonian vision, and immediately follows with an extraordinary power encounter with the Python spirit and a supernatural release from jail during the first European missionary target—Philippi.

Instead of Jesus appearing to Paul in the vision as He did on the Damascus road, this time God shows Paul a Macedonian man saying, **"Come over to Macedonia and help us"** (v. 9). This sovereign call of God also fits, to some extent, the missiological criteria we have mentioned on which Paul had been planning his evangelistic strategy—Greek-speaking cities that had large Jewish populations. In this case, the people of Macedonia, although ruled by the Romans, spoke Greek. The downside was that Philippi, the chief city of Macedonia, had only a small Jewish population, not a large one. Nevertheless, the missionaries **immediately [seek] to go to Macedonia** (v. 10).

Welcome, Dr. Luke

Luke, the author of Acts, says that **after [Paul] had seen the vision, immediately *we* sought to go to Macedonia** (v. 10, italics added). Changing from the third person to the first person, from "they" to "we," indicates that at this point Luke apparently joins the missionary team.

Through the many years I have studied the Acts of the

Apostles, I have developed a human-interest hypothesis about the life of Dr. Luke that I have not yet found in any of the commentaries. That, some would say, should be reason enough for me not to mention it. They base such an assumption on a notion that so many scholars have written so many commentaries on Acts—1,398 commentaries to be exact—that every possible explanation of events underlying the text must at some time or other have already been suggested. I do not, however, necessarily agree with this assumption. My alternate assumption is that each of the now-standard interpretations of the passages in Acts must have originated sometime in the past with a new suggestion by a certain individual or individuals who had not previously seen it in any of the then-existing commentaries. Therefore, I do not have any particular inhibition to keep me from stepping out from time to time and risk my own interpretation. Readers of *Lighting the World* may recall that I did just that when I hypothesized that the evidence in Acts 11 would indicate the possibility of *two* missions to Antioch, not one. One mission was to the Jews in Antioch and the other (which I called the Cyprus and Cyrene Mission [CCM]) was specifically targeting the Gentiles.

The Life of Biblical Scholars

For those who are unfamiliar with the daily lives of biblical scholars, let me explain. These are highly educated people who have made a profession of studying and teaching the Bible. The subject of their studies is 66 relatively short books, so it is a much more limited field than, say, astronomy, Chinese history or computer science might be. Furthermore, their scholarly predecessors have been studying and interpreting the same 66 books for almost 20 centuries. It is not surprising, then, that one of the desires of biblical scholars is to offer a first-time hypothesis that will throw some new light on the biblical text and that will hopefully elicit agreement from some other scholars in the field.

By doing this, the scholars are also mentally prepared for the eventuality that some colleagues may disagree. A certain vocabulary is commonly used in such discussions. When one agrees with the new hypothesis it is lauded as "exegesis," meaning it appears to have been drawn from the biblical text. This is seen as legitimate. If one disagrees, it will commonly be termed "eisegesis," meaning that the hypothesis is not demanded by the text, but has been superimposed onto the text by the author. This is not considered legitimate. Sometimes the boundary line between the two is not all that clear.

By way of illustration, consider the opinions of recognized biblical scholars regarding the passage in Acts 16:10, in which Luke begins to write in the first person, "we." Most scholars agree that the passage was written by Luke, but others suggest it may more likely be an insertion by Luke of something written by Paul, Silas or Timothy. Most scholars think that Luke met Paul in Troas, and others surmise that he might actually have been traveling with Paul ever since they left Antioch. And how did Luke and Paul meet? Here are some of the scholars' hypotheses:

- Paul was sick in Galatia, so when he arrived in Troas he decided to find a good doctor.
- Luke looked for Paul because he had heard many stories of Paul's ministry of faith healing and was curious to know more about it.
- Luke was the Macedonian man whom Paul had seen in the vision, so Paul recognized him when he later saw him in Troas.
- Luke had talked to Paul about the challenge of Macedonia, thus priming Paul for the vision he was to have.[3]

Are these suggestions "exegesis" or "eisegesis?"

Did Luke Marry Lydia?

Two of the major characters in this missionary episode in Philippi are Luke and Lydia. Luke, as I described in detail in *Spreading the Fire*, was a physician and, like many physicians, was in all probability cultured, well educated, widely traveled and wealthy. Lydia is described as **a seller of purple from the city of Thyatira** (v. 14), which casts her in the role of an international merchant. David W. J. Gill, a New Testament scholar, draws from several sources to suggest that Lydia was "of some standing" socially, a member of the "social elite," a seller of "luxury items or exotic merchandise, such as purple dye or perfumes"[4] and wealthy. In other words, like Luke, Lydia was cultured, well educated, widely traveled and wealthy. They were both Gentiles. Could it be that they were both single? According to Bradley Blue, the fact that Lydia was the owner of her own large home makes it quite likely, although not certain, that she was single.[5]

Here is where the human interest comes in. After many exciting events in Philippi, which we will see in detail shortly, the last place we find the missionaries, Paul, Silas, Timothy and Luke, is in the house of Lydia where they had been lodged. But when they leave Philippi, the "we" suddenly changes to "they"! Luke obviously stayed behind. Did he stay lodged in Lydia's house? Could they have decided to marry each other and help form the nucleus of that wonderful church in Philippi that later sent substantial financial gifts to Paul and his missionary team? When Paul later wrote a letter to the church at Philippi and mentioned his "true companion" (Phil. 4:3), could that be a reference to Luke? Several commentators, F. F. Bruce among them, think it might well have been Luke.[6]

Just a hypothesis!

Targeting the Synagogue Community

··

16:13. On the Sabbath day we went out of the city to the riverside, where prayer was customarily made; and we sat down and spoke to the women who met there.
14. Now a certain woman named Lydia heard us. She was a seller of purple from Thyatira, who worshiped God. The Lord opened her heart to heed the things spoken by Paul.

··

As I have mentioned, Philippi did not have a large Jewish population. It did not even have a synagogue. In those days, a proper synagogue required at least 10 adult Jewish males for its nucleus, and apparently that many Jewish males did not reside in Philippi. So instead of attending a synagogue, the Jewish women in Philippi customarily observed the Sabbath by gathering at a spot near the river to pray together. Although not a synagogue, such a gathering was, nevertheless, a functional substitute for a synagogue.

One of these women was Lydia, **who worshiped God.** She was not a Jew, but a Gentile attracted to the true God of the Jews, better known as a "God-fearer." The typical synagogue community would likely be composed of Jews, proselytes and God-fearers. Proselytes had been born Gentiles, but they had broken their ties with their Gentile culture and had officially converted to Judaism. From that point on, they were regarded by all, not as Gentiles, but as bona fide Jews. They were called "proselytes" to distinguish them from biological Jews. The God-fearers were also born Gentiles but they had not yet decided to take the step of conversion through circumcision of the males, baptism and subjection to the Jewish law. They remained Gentiles, but were admitted to the fringes of the synagogue community under certain restrictions.

Paul's established evangelistic strategy was to head directly for the synagogue community in any new city on his ministry itinerary. He later did this in Thessalonica (see Acts 17:1), in Berea (see v. 10), in Athens (see v. 17), in Corinth (see 18:4) and in Ephesus (see 19:8). He went to the synagogues because there he would find the most receptive people for the gospel message he was bringing to them.

The Jews themselves were not particularly receptive, although we have records of a number of them deciding to follow Jesus as Messiah as Paul went from city to city. Indeed, in Corinth two synagogue presidents, no less, were converted. Proselytes would be the least likely to convert because they had paid such a high personal price to become Jews that going back would not ordinarily be an attractive option. A serious problem for all Jews, whether ethnic Jews or proselytes, was Paul's willingness to admit Gentiles into the "people of God" without demanding circumcision. Strictly orthodox Jews could not so much as tolerate such a thought.

God-Fearers Were Ready for the Gospel

Those who were most receptive to the gospel were the God-fearers such as Lydia. Paul's message to them would have been something like: "Do you want to know and follow the true God? Are you here in the synagogue community because you realize that He is the God whom the Jews worship? Have these synagogue leaders told you that to know God and be fully accepted by Him you first must be circumcised, become a Jew and obey the Jewish law? Well, I have come with good news for you. God loves you and He sent the Messiah, Jesus Christ, to die for you on the cross. Through faith in Jesus, God will forgive your sins, restore you to fellowship with Himself, and welcome you into His family. And all this while you remain a Gentile as you always have been."

The God-fearers had been waiting for exactly this kind of a message! When they heard and understood Paul's message, many of them opened their hearts to Christ and were born again. Then, because they had not previously broken cultural and social contact with their fellow Gentiles, they could easily move among Gentiles who were not God-fearers and bring them the message of salvation. At this point in particular, the mighty signs and wonders that ordinarily accompanied the preaching of the gospel message had maximum impact. First-century evangelism was consistently a combination of word and deed.

The result of this missionary strategy was multiplying Christian churches that were predominantly Gentile churches. Paul's original commission from the Lord on the Damascus road involved this very thing. Jesus had said He was sending Paul to the *Gentiles* "**to open their eyes, in order to turn them from darkness to light, and from the power of Satan to God**" (26:18). Paul self-identified as an apostle to the uncircumcised (see Gal. 2:7,8).

Lydia and Group Conversion

> **16:15. And when she [Lydia] and her household were baptized, she begged us, saying, "If you have judged me to be faithful to the Lord, come to my house and stay." So she persuaded us.**

Not only was Lydia an outstanding example of a God-fearer prepared to receive the gospel, but all her household also came to Christ at the same time she did. Who were the people in her household? The lack of any reference to a husband is further indication that Lydia could have been single at the time.

Whether she had previously been married is not known. If she had been, it would be expected that any children would have also been part of her household. Other close relatives might have been living with her. And because she was a woman of means, she would have had a household staff of servants or slaves. When Lydia as the head of the household decided to convert to Christianity, the rest of her household would naturally be expected to follow suit.

Group conversion is difficult for many of us Westerners to comprehend or to consider as fully legitimate. Worldwide, America has gained the reputation of being an extremely individualistic culture. Our frontier mind-set and the expectation that all of us must pull ourselves up by our own bootstraps if we expect to be successful seems like a distorted value system to at least two-thirds of today's global population.

In most parts of the world, all *important* decisions are made by groups. Because only insignificant decisions are left to individuals, when missionaries come with an individualistic gospel, it frequently seems as though it must be an unimportant issue to those they are trying to win. Of course, Western missionaries often attach a theological reason to insisting that each person make his or her own decision. "Dare to be a Daniel; dare to stand alone" is the watchword of many. I recall that as a young man, I first decided whom I was going to marry, and *then* informed my parents. Although to us this may not seem like unusual behavior, to most people in the world it is utterly preposterous. People simply do not make such important decisions on their own.

The times of many people turning to Christ throughout history have been by what missiologists call "people movements to Christ." They are defined as *multi-individual, mutually interdependent conversions.* That is what happened, quite naturally, in Lydia's household. The resultant professions of faith in that era were just as valid as people being saved one by one in a Billy Graham meeting today.

We see major people movements occurring in China and India in our time. A people movement has been ignited among Korean-Americans, in which we find that 70 percent of Koreans living in the United States are Christians compared to only 25 percent of Koreans living in Korea. If, for example, we ever successfully evangelize our Native-American Indian population, it will have to come largely, if not almost exclusively, through people movements in each tribal network. Lydia and her household experiencing group conversion should be more of a model for us today than it often seems to be.

High-Level Power Encounter

16. Now it happened, as we went to prayer, that a certain slave girl possessed with a spirit of divination met us, who brought her masters much profit by fortune-telling.
17. This girl followed Paul and us, and cried out, saying, "These men are the servants of the Most High God, who proclaim to us the way of salvation."
18. And this she did for many days. But Paul, greatly annoyed, turned and said to the spirit, "I command you in the name of Jesus Christ to come out of her." And he came out that very hour.

The book of Acts contains four, possibly five, incidents of high-level spiritual warfare:

1. Peter's encounter with the sorcerer Simon Magus in

Samaria, of whom was said, "This man is the great power of God" (8:10).

2. Paul's encounter with Bar-Jesus (or Elymas) who was employed as a medium by the Roman proconsul of Cyprus, Sergius Paulus (see 13:6-12).

3. The event in Philippi in which Paul confronts the Python spirit (see 16:16-18).

4. Breaking the power of Diana of the Ephesians (see ch. 19), which we shall see later in chapter 5.

5. The fifth incident, which possibly fits into the same set, would be the encounter between King Herod, who had ordered Peter's execution, and the prayer warriors in the house of Mary the mother of Mark (see 12:1-23).

Although it is also mentioned in the first two volumes in this Acts series, it will be helpful to review once again the terminology for the three major levels of spiritual warfare:

Ground-level spiritual warfare means casting demons out of individuals.

Occult-level spiritual warfare involves dealing with the demonic forces active in spiritism, witchcraft, New Age, shamanism, freemasonry, satanism and other forms of the occult.

Strategic-level spiritual warfare. Some prefer to call this cosmic-level spiritual warfare because it deals with high-ranking principalities and powers or territorial spirits that have been assigned the responsibility of keeping people of a given geographical area or social network in darkness.

We should keep in mind that these three categories are simply conceptual devices to help us understand more clearly some of the complex aspects of the battles in the invisible world. The lines between the three are not sharp and clear. Much of it overlaps, and, furthermore, spiritual warfare on any one of the three levels has repercussions in varying degrees through the other two because we are invading the same kingdom of darkness.

A thoughtful question has been raised by some people whether these four or five stories about spiritual warfare in Acts actually reach into the area of strategic-level spiritual warfare. It has been argued that the incidents involving people such as Simon Magus in Samaria, Bar-Jesus in Cyprus and the slave girl in Philippi could better be seen as ground-level, or, because all three were occult practitioners, perhaps occult-level spiritual warfare. And Paul himself, as we will see, never directly confronted Diana of the Ephesians. His encounter with the magicians in Ephesus would clearly have been considered occult-level spiritual warfare.

The Question of Authority

The reason some people raise these questions is because of a theological assumption—namely that Christians are given authority to deal with demons that are attached to a person, but are not given similar authority to deal with evil spirits at other levels or in other spheres. Because this is a crucial issue in the contemporary dialogue about spiritual warfare, I am going to reproduce here a paragraph from the A.D. 2000 United Prayer Track Philosophy of Prayer statement that attempts to state the differences in as clear terms as possible:

16. Our Sphere of Authority

One of the most prominent unresolved issues among members of the Spiritual Warfare Network is on which, if any, of the three levels we are given biblical authority for intentional ministry. We appreciate the fact that much more dialogue on this matter is in order. Some feel that because the principal biblical examples we have of spiritual warfare involve casting demons out of individuals, we should not advocate engaging spiritual forces which may be occupying geographical areas or buildings or animals or human social networks or churches or physical objects such as trees or mountains or idols. For them it is not advisable to do strategic-level warfare and name, rebuke or otherwise address so-called territorial spirits. Others prefer to give a literal interpretation to such sayings of Jesus as "Behold, I give you the authority...over all the power of the enemy" (Lk. 10:19) and do confrontive spiritual warfare on all levels (see Col. 1:16-20, Jn. 16:15). All desire to see the captives of the Enemy set free.[7]

As readers of this Acts series and of my previous *Prayer Warrior* series will know, I join those who take literally Jesus' words that He has given us authority "over *all* the power of the enemy" (Luke 10:19, italics added). It is also my opinion that Paul mentions the sword of the Spirit, the Word of God, in his description of our struggle with principalities in Ephesians 6:12-18 because we are to use the sword in the struggle against them. It is my view that sound missiological strategy will take responsible, but aggressive, action to bind demonic strong ones, principalities, powers, territorial spirits, or whatever they might be called, who are serving Satan by keeping large populations in spiritual darkness. I also believe that such was Paul's understanding of Jesus' command to him **to open their [the Gentiles'] eyes, in order to turn them from darkness to light, and from the power of Satan to God** (Acts 26:18).

In my opinion, Luke's accounts of Simon Magus, Bar-Jesus and the demonized slave girl in Philippi could each be reasonably understood as involving strategic-level spiritual warfare. I base this on the assumption that territorial spirits from time to time can and do choose to manifest in the natural world by demonizing certain people.

Field reports from many who are engaged in frontline spiritual warfare have confirmed this assumption. One of the best-known reports is what Lester Sumrall calls "the greatest battle of my life" when he cast a demon out of a witch named Clarita Villanueva in Bilibid Prison in the Philippines in 1986. Why would I suggest that this might have been a territorial spirit? The extremely unusual power of the spirit itself could have been one indication. But even more, history shows that the spiritual climate of the Philippines changed significantly at that point. The rate of evangelism and church multiplication in the Philippines since 1986 greatly surpasses anything seen previously.[8]

Power encounters with Simon Magus and Bar-Jesus likewise changed the spiritual climates of Samaria and Cyprus respectively. Luke reports that in Samaria **both men and women were baptized (8:12)** and in Cyprus **the proconsul believed, when he saw what had been done, being astonished at the teaching of the Lord (13:12).** Whether in the Philippines, Samaria or Cyprus, these power encounters seem to involve something substantially different from what occurs in the ordinary ground-level deliverance ministries in which people are freed from afflicting spirits. In such cases, the ripple effect of deliverance might be felt among immediate family and friends, but that is far short of seeing entire geographical areas undergo spiritual transformation and increasing receptivity to the gospel. At such a point, understanding spiritual warfare accurately becomes significant for missiology and world evangelization.

I have chosen to develop this issue at some length because this incident in Philippi is the clearest example we have in Acts of direct confrontation with a territorial spirit. Incidents later in Ephesus produce more evangelistic fruit, but they do not involve direct confrontation such as occurs here in Philippi.

A Demonized Slave Girl

....

16. ...a certain slave girl possessed with a spirit of
divination met us, who brought her masters much
profit by fortune-telling.

....

The owners of this slave girl may have known or cared little about the supernatural forces at work, but they cared very much about the substantial income they were receiving through her services. How was it that they could make so much money through this fortune-teller?

The obvious answer is that this slave girl was good at fortune-telling. She knew the future, and she had built a sound reputation for accuracy. Any number of other fortune-tellers in Philippi must not have been making as much money because they simply weren't as good. The slave girl had not gained her stature in the occult community by making constant mistakes.

Another question that surfaces in some minds is whether this girl's ability was true supernatural power or just superstition. I have found this word "superstition" carelessly used by some otherwise thoughtful Christians. To say, for example, that consulting a spiritist medium such as this girl is "superstition" tends to imply that we are dealing with psychological issues rather than issues of real supernatural power. My dictionary says that "superstition" means "an irrational belief in or notion of the ominous significance of a particular thing, circumstance, occurrence."[9] The ordinary person thinks that superstition might be a fear of walking under ladders or black cats crossing our paths, something not worth paying much attention to because these are most likely figments of the imagination. The words on the paper slips in Chinese fortune cookies might be another example of this kind of superstition, but these certainly do not compare to the kind of fortune-telling the slave girl was practicing in Philippi.

This slave girl was serving as a channel for actual supernatural power. The spirits of darkness in Philippi could reveal to her many things that would occur in the future simply because they at the time had considerable control over the entire society, and they had the power to determine much of what would happen in the future. John said, "The whole world lies under the sway of the wicked one" (1 John 5:19). He also writes that through Jesus "the true light is already shining" (2:8) and that those of us who are following Jesus "have overcome the wicked one" (v. 13). Only through the light of the world—Jesus Christ—can the control of Satan and his forces of darkness be weakened and dispelled. But before Paul and the other missionaries had arrived in Philippi, darkness was in full control of much of the future. This is why fortune-telling could be amazingly accurate.

Also notice that if cities such as Philippi were indeed under the control of demonic beings, it might not be inaccurate to regard the higher-ranking ones as territorial spirits. And, as we shall see, the particular spirit empowering the slave girl happened to be one of the big ones. Those who understood the power of such demonic forces were not irrational or superstitious. Their rational minds had accurately perceived the reality of the spiritual power with which they were dealing—in this case, the Python spirit.

The Python Spirit

The slave girl in Philippi was demonized with a **spirit of divination** (Acts 16:16). Our English Bible versions translate the Greek *pneuma pythona* by using the *functional* name of this spirit, "spirit of divination" or "spirit of clairvoyance," instead of the *proper* name, "Python spirit." When we attempt to identify demonic beings in general, we frequently use the one or the other.

In Latin America, for example, one of the most powerful and pervasive spirits is a spirit of religion well entrenched in the Roman Catholic church, which for centuries has kept multitudes in spiritual darkness by deceiving them into thinking they would be saved by their religion. "Spirit of religion" is the functional name of this high-ranking demon. Its proper name, according to those engaged in spiritual mapping in Latin America, is "Queen of Heaven," mentioned in the Bible in Jeremiah 7:18. Working as a spirit of religion, the Queen of Heaven has apparently succeeded in disguising herself very skillfully as the Virgin Mary, and has thereby delighted in receiving the worship of millions. Mentioning this is neither to deny that many Latin American Roman Catholics are sincere born-again Christians serving the Lord, nor to ignore the fact that the true historic Mary, mother of Jesus, is "blessed...among women" (Luke 1:28). It is simply to illustrate the difference between functional and proper names of demonic spirits by using a familiar case study.

In my opinion, it would have been better to translate *pneuma pythona* literally as "Python spirit." Simon Kistemaker argues that the best way to translates it into English is: "a spirit, namely, a Python."[10] This helps us form a clearer picture of why it is feasible to treat this as a case of strategic-level spiritual warfare. We realize much more precisely with what Paul was actually dealing.

Who was Python? R. C. H. Lenski says it was "the mythical serpent or dragon that dwelt in the region Pytho at the foot of the Parnassus in Phocis and was said to have guarded the oracle at Delphi until it was slain by the god Apollo."[11] Delphi was the city in Greece in which a famous temple of Apollo was located, the seat of the Delphic oracle. Apollo was a powerful demonic spirit of prophecy who spoke on behalf of the great king of the gods, Zeus (Greek) or Jupiter (Roman).

Delphi was no ordinary Greek city. Here is how Everett

Ferguson describes it: "According to legend Zeus wanted to determine the center of the earth, so he released two eagles from opposite ends of the world. They met over Delphi. The omphalos stone at Delphi marked the navel of the earth, and Delphi became the spiritual center of the Greek world." Ferguson goes on to say that Delphi was a "cult center of the earth goddess," "the center of Apollo's worship," and "The main attraction of Delphi was its oracle, located under the temple of Apollo."[12]

What was an oracle? An oracle was a religious institution focused upon an individual who had a satanically empowered gift of prophecy and who was sought out by many who wished to determine the will of the spirits. The oracle at Delphi was a priestess known as the Pythia because she was empowered by the Python spirit. According to Ferguson, she would only prophecy on the seventh day of each month when she would take a ceremonial bath, sacrifice a goat to Apollo, enter an underground chamber beneath the temple and sit on Apollo's tripod. Those who wished to receive her words would pay a high monetary price.[13]

A first-century spiritual mapper might well designate Delphi as the seat of Satan for Greece. Paul had encountered this same Python spirit as a spirit of divination in the slave girl at Philippi. This is what makes me suggest we have a description of something more than simple ground-level spiritual warfare.

Python's Theology Was Accurate

....

16:17. This girl followed Paul and us, and cried out, saying, "These men are the servants of the Most High God, who proclaim to us the way of salvation."

....

We should keep in mind that these words are not those of the slave girl, but of the evil spirit that had taken control of her. The Python spirit's theology happened to be accurate. He recognized that the missionaries were true representatives of God, and that their message of salvation was true. Demons are inveterate liars, but not everything they say is a lie. Whether they speak the truth or falsehoods, however, their ultimate goal is to deceive. Sometimes they deceive by first building false credibility. The Python spirit spoke true theology and told true fortunes, enchanting people much as a spider would invite a fly into its web.

Mark tells of a spirit that once tried to pacify Jesus by saying, "I know who You are—the Holy One of God" (Mark 1:24). But Jesus wasn't impressed. "Jesus rebuked him, saying, 'Be quiet, and come out of him!'" (v. 25). I like what James says about this: "You believe that there is one God. You do well. Even the demons believe—and tremble!" (Jas. 2:19).

Paul Pulls the Trigger

16:18. And this she did for many days. But Paul, greatly annoyed, turned and said to the spirit, "I command you in the name of Jesus Christ to come out of her." And he came out that very hour.

This example of a direct, high-level power encounter has two important aspects:

1. *Paul's method.* Paul addressed the spirit directly.
2. *Paul's timing.* Paul did not cast out the spirit when it first manifested, but only after several days.

This raises two significant questions for us. Should we, like Paul, address spirits directly, or only address God? If we should address the spirits, how long should we wait before confronting them?

Should We Address Spirits?

The question whether we should address spirits directly or whether we should only pray to God and ask Him to deal with them frequently is often raised in discussions of strategic-level spiritual warfare.

Usually, it soon becomes clear that this question is not ordinarily asked in relationship to ground-level spiritual warfare. The overwhelming consensus of those who are active in deliverance ministries involving power encounters is that demons can and should be told to leave. I just referred to Jesus' deliverance of the demonized man in the synagogue where He directly addressed the spirit, saying, "Be quiet, and come out of him!" (Mark 1:25).

I realize, of course, that some people approach individual deliverance from the viewpoint of the *truth encounter* rather than the *power encounter*. Even in cases where people seek freedom in Christ through truth encounter, however, they frequently end up informing the demons directly who they really are in Christ's kingdom, thereby serving the spirits an eviction notice, which the demons usually obey. A major proponent of this methodology is Neil Anderson, author of the excellent book *Victory over the Darkness* (Regal Books).

One of the Scripture references many people use to argue that even if demons may be directly addressed on ground level, they should not be so addressed on the strategic level is Jude 9: "Yet Michael the archangel, in contending with the devil, when he disputed about the body of Moses, dared not bring against him a reviling accusation, but said, 'The Lord rebuke you!'"

Several things need to be mentioned in referring to Jude 9.

First, Jude 9 is not written in the context of methodologies of spiritual warfare, but in a passage teaching that we should not go beyond the bounds of whatever authority God has given to us.

Second, Jude 9 condemns godless, immoral men (see vv. 4,8) who *slander* (rather than *rebuke* under Christ's authority) angelic beings.

Third, the text deals with addressing Satan himself, not lesser spirits such as Python.

Fourth, it refers to Old Testament times before Jesus had given His disciples authority "over all the power of the enemy" (Luke 10:19). New Testament authority is quite different.

Fifth, it is a strange text, based on something from the apocryphal book of First Enoch. The Old Testament tells us nothing of a "body of Moses." Granted, it is Scripture, but basing important teaching on Jude 9 would be as risky as basing important teaching on the passage in 1 Corinthians 15:29, which speaks of the custom of "baptizing the dead." For these reasons, I do not believe Jude 9 gives us sufficient evidence to limit our proactive spiritual warfare to lower-ranking demons.

Paul's direct address to the Python spirit is evidence enough for many, me included, that God does direct us to speak with the authority of the name of Jesus to territorial spirits, and that it should be seen as acceptable Christian protocol to do so. Mary spoke directly to the angel Gabriel (see Luke 1:34), and Jesus spoke directly to the Legion spirit (see Mark 5:8,9). The psalmist also spoke directly to demonic principalities in Psalm 97:7, "Worship Him, all you gods," and in 29:1, "Give unto the Lord, O you mighty ones, give unto the Lord glory and strength."

Why Did Paul Wait?

It is puzzling to some that Paul allowed the Python spirit to manifest **for many days** (Acts 16:18) before casting it out. I am sure this is best explained by crediting Paul with following one of the most basic rules of strategic-level spiritual warfare: *proceed only on God's timing*. If it is true that God gives us the authority to deal with principalities and powers, it is equally true that we had better proceed only on cue from God Himself.

Jesus set the pattern for us when He said, "Most assuredly, I say to you, the Son can do nothing of Himself, but what He sees the Father do" (John 5:19). If Jesus had to check His timing in ministry with the Father, so we much more must do the same. That is why prayer is important in spiritual warfare. Prayer establishes the intimacy we need with the Father so that He can communicate clearly to us and let us know exactly what His timing might be.

Although this is speculation, I think it made good sense for God to postpone the final deliverance for several days while the tension about the fortune-teller was building and Paul was becoming **greatly annoyed** (Acts 16:18). Furthermore, it allowed the intercessors more time to weaken the spirit through prayer. This episode of strategic-level spiritual warfare would affect the whole city of Philippi. Therefore, the more public the battle the better. If Paul had cast out the Python spirit the first day, few would have known about it. But when it finally happened, it turned out to be a major public display of the power of God over the power of Satan, and the territorial spirit over Philippi was thoroughly embarrassed. The strongman had been bound in the name of Jesus. The way had been opened for the gospel to spread and for a powerful church to be planted.

A Vicious Counterattack

19. But when her masters saw that their hope of
profit was gone, they seized Paul and Silas and dragged
them into the marketplace to the authorities.
20. And they brought them to the magistrates, and said,

"These men, being Jews, exceedingly trouble our city;
21. and they teach customs which are not lawful for us,
being Romans, to receive or observe."
22. Then the multitude rose up together against them;
and the magistrates tore off their clothes and commanded
them to be beaten with rods.
23. And when they had laid many stripes on them, they
threw them into prison, commanding the jailer to keep
them securely.

Many avoid confronting spiritual powers of darkness because they fear a possible counterattack. Such fear is well grounded. The notion of Christian immunity to satanic attacks is a fanciful hope rather than an accurate evaluation of spiritual reality. Here we have a vivid example of missionaries engaging the enemy on a high level, undeterred by what must have been a frank appraisal of the potential risk involved. Paul was not a novice. He definitely was a spiritual warrior who did not love his life to the death (see Rev. 12:11).

In this case, the missionaries were arrested, beaten with rods and thrown into jail. Civil punishment by beating, or caning as some call it, is considered cruel and unusual punishment in the United States, and, therefore, it is hard for Americans to comprehend the intense physical agony Paul and Silas would be suffering as they were thrown into their jail cell. People in Singapore and other parts of the world where criminals receive physical punishment understand it well. Was binding the strongman over the city worth it?

The masters of the fortune-teller must have been influential citizens of Philippi, explained undoubtedly by their relationship with supernatural powers and bolstered by their considerable wealth. Their underlying motive for attacking Paul and Silas was financial. They **saw that their hope of profit was gone** (Acts

16:19). They were out of business. Why? Their fortune-teller could no longer tell fortunes accurately, and she may have been the first to admit it. The Python spirit who had given her the knowledge had left her. This in itself should dispel any remaining doubt that she had told correct fortunes because of the supernatural power she had channeled, and that we are not here reading about some irrational "superstition."

The public charges against the missionaries were, of course, along different lines. Political charges of confusion and civil unrest along with cultural charges of teaching illicit customs were brought against the missionaries. An anti-Semitic flavor was added in highlighting that they were Jews. It is interesting that neither Timothy nor Luke, who were not full-blooded Jews, were persecuted.

Warfare Is Not for All

Christians should realize that suffering comes with the territory of being a Christian and serving God in His kingdom. Peter makes this clear when he writes, "Beloved, do not think it strange concerning the fiery trial which is to try you, as though some strange thing happened to you; but rejoice to the extent that you partake of Christ's sufferings" (1 Pet. 4:12,13). This is not a welcome Scripture for many of us. We tend to be more readily attracted to promises of health, freedom, prosperity and peace, all combining for the trouble-free Christian life. Some Christians believe they are entitled to all this. These amenities are certainly part of God's kingdom and included in His promises, but we might not attain them all in this life because we have not yet pushed back the enemy. When Paul and Silas lay beat up and bleeding on the filthy floor of the Philippi jail, they probably had as much faith and were as doctrinally sound and as filled with the Holy Spirit as Christians should be. But they had no trouble-free Christian life!

This is not to say that all Christians have a divine calling to penetrate the darkness of unreached people groups where Satan is still at the peak of his malignant power. Few of us will ever walk in the footsteps of Paul and Silas, although some will. Many believers are called by the same God to do other things. One pastor I know says that God has called His church to be a "bedroom" rather than a "battlefield." Some need protection rather than warfare, and they are reluctant to "duke it out with the devil." John Mark apparently was one of them. If he thought the battle with Bar-Jesus in Cyprus was bad, imagine how he might have reacted to confronting the Python spirit here in Philippi. Yet, Mark has gone down in history as a hero of the Christian faith.

Martin Luther said it well when he wrote the famous song "A Mighty Fortress Is Our God":[14]

> *Let goods and kindred go,*
> *This mortal life also—*
> *The body they may kill;*
> *God's truth abideth still:*
> *His kingdom is forever.*

The Second Power Encounter

....

16:24. Having received such a charge, he put them into
the inner prison and fastened their feet in the stocks.
25. But at midnight Paul and Silas were praying
and singing hymns to God, and the prisoners
were listening to them.
26. Suddenly there was a great earthquake,
so that the foundations of the prison were shaken; and
immediately all the doors were opened and everyone's
chains were loosed.

....

Humanly speaking, the situation was hopeless. Paul and Silas were not just in jail, but they were also in the innermost cell, physically beaten, exhausted and bleeding, their hands chained and their feet in stocks. Although no visible way of escape was open to them, they had come to Europe with power and they knew that the major weapons in the spiritual battle they had engaged in with the enemy were prayer and praise.

Instead of giving up, they slept the best they could under the circumstances. At midnight they were not only wide awake, but they were also singing praises to God! They did not complain that God had somehow let them down, but they exalted God for the privilege of serving Him and suffering for the advance of His kingdom. Praise should be seen as a form of prayer. Jesus told us to start our prayers by saying "Hallowed be Your name" (Matt. 6:9), which is a word of praise to God. Paul and Silas were singing praises to an audience of one—God. The other prisoners were mere eavesdroppers.

Relatively few believers recognize that praise in itself is one of the most powerful weapons of spiritual warfare we have at our disposition. Scripture says that God inhabits the praises of His people (see Ps. 22:3). The devil cannot long resist praises to God. In Philippi, the major spiritual battle against Python had been won. The forces of darkness were now harassing Paul and Silas with a caning and imprisonment, but they could not maintain their ground in the face of praise and worship. In this case, without any overt confrontation with the forces of darkness, deliverance came.

Deliverance came in the form of an unusual earthquake. I say unusual because I live in California where we experience many earthquakes. How an earthquake could loosen all the chains of all the prisoners inside the jail without toppling the structure itself is a question that even the seismologists at The California Institute of Technology would undoubtedly have a difficult time explaining. Loosening one or two chains, maybe. But all the

chains without harming any of the prisoners? Only a very specific action of God synchronized with the general shaking of the
earth could possibly account for what had happened. It was clearly an answer to prayer, not just a coincidental natural phenomenon. Once again, the power of God was seen in Philippi.

Consoling the Jailer

16:27. And the keeper of the prison, awaking from sleep
and seeing the prison doors open, supposing the prisoners
had fled, drew his sword and was about to kill himself.
28. But Paul called with a loud voice, saying,
"Do yourself no harm, for we are all here."
29. Then he called for a light, ran in, and fell down
trembling before Paul and Silas.

The jailer was ready to commit suicide, but Paul intervened and
stopped him. The jailer had no need to kill himself because none
of the prisoners under his charge had left the jail. When the jailer went into the prison, he singled out Paul and Silas. Why? Out
of all the prisoners in the jail, how did he know that Paul and
Silas had been key players in the drama that had unfolded?

The jailer was undoubtedly aware that some kind of extraordinary spiritual power was involved in this entire scenario. By the
time he had been taken to jail, Paul had gained a citywide public
reputation for ministering in the power of God. Everyone, including the jailer, would have known about Paul's decisive victory
over the Python spirit and the fury of the fortune-teller's masters
who were responsible for Paul's being in jail. By now, the jailer
would have been sure that Paul and Silas represented the true
God, and he now wanted to have a part in what they were doing.

The Fruit of Warfare

> 30. And he brought them out and said,
> "Sirs, what must I do to be saved?"
> 31. So they said, "Believe on the Lord Jesus Christ,
> and you will be saved, you and your household."
> 32. Then they spoke the word of the Lord to
> him and to all who were in his house.
> 33. And he took them the same hour of the night
> and washed their stripes. And immediately he and
> all his family were baptized.

It is important, in my opinion, to keep reminding ourselves of the true purpose of strategic-level spiritual warfare. Binding territorial spirits is not an end in itself, but only a means to the end of freeing the captives under their control so that unsaved people can hear the gospel and be saved. As Paul would later write, "But even if our gospel is veiled, it is veiled to those who are perishing, whose minds the god of this age has blinded, who do not believe, lest the light of the gospel of the glory of Christ, who is the image of God, should shine on them" (2 Cor. 4:3,4). No one was ever saved by binding the strong one. Salvation comes only through believing the gospel of Christ. But binding the strong one frees lost people to choose whether or not they will believe, though previously Satan had their minds blinded. In Philippi, Satan had apparently delegated this evil work to the Python spirit.

Note that, as in the case of Lydia, we have here another example of group conversion. **Immediately he [the jailer] and all his family were baptized** (Acts 16:33). Presumably, the household group that was baptized included not only the relatives, but also the slaves, which in all probability they would have owned.

These new converts were baptized immediately. We are not told that Paul or any of the missionaries did the baptizing. It could well have been that the missionaries had assigned this to the Philippian believers, new in the faith as they were, so that baptisms would be a part of normal church life after the missionaries left. The best missionary strategy stresses incorporating the new converts into local churches as quickly as possible.

Jesus tells His disciples, "Go therefore and make disciples of all the nations, baptizing them in the name of the Father and of the Son and of the Holy Spirit" (Matt. 28:19). If evangelism is equivalent to making disciples and not just preaching or passing out tracts, incorporation into the local church will not be seen as some afterthought, but as part and parcel of the evangelistic strategy itself. This, I think, is what Jesus had in mind in the Great Commission just cited, and it was Paul's procedure on the mission field.

Moving On

35. And when it was day, the magistrates sent
the officers, saying, "Let those men go."
37. But Paul said to them, "They have beaten us openly,
uncondemned Romans, and have thrown us into prison.
And now do they put us out secretly? No indeed! Let
them come themselves and get us out."

God had opened the doors of the jail, but Paul did not become a fugitive. He chose to remain in the jail. But when the authorities tried to free him, Paul demanded a public showdown. This was now a matter of civil justice. Roman citizens deserved a trial before punishment, but Paul and Silas, both Roman citizens, had been beaten and jailed illegally. The city leaders were obviously in trouble:

> 38. And the officers told these words to the magistrates, and they were afraid when they heard that they were Romans.
> 39. Then they came and pleaded with them and brought them out, and asked them to depart from the city.

After receiving the apology, Paul apparently did not think he should press charges of wrongful punishment. His time in Philippi was coming to a close and he was ready to move on.

> 40. So they went out of the prison and entered the house of Lydia; and when they had seen the brethren, they encouraged them and departed.

As I mentioned earlier in this chapter, it is rather fascinating that the last place we see the missionaries in Philippi is in Lydia's house, and when they leave, Luke's narrative suddenly switches from "we" to "they." Paul, Silas and Timothy continued their missionary work on new frontiers. Luke stayed behind in Lydia's house. Of course, the romantic notion I earlier proposed, that Luke and Lydia might have married, cannot be definitively proved or disproved by the text itself.

Reflection Questions

1. Paul and his friends missed hearing accurately from God when they set out first for Asia and then for Bithynia. Can

you think of similar experiences of your own where you found you were going in the wrong direction?

2. Talk about the possibility that Luke might have married Lydia in Philippi. On a probability scale of 1 to 10, where would you place it? Why?

3. What is your view on the authority given to believers over demonic powers? Is it limited to casting out demons from people or does it also involve higher demonic forces?

4. Warfare against the Python spirit in Philippi caused Paul and Silas great suffering. Are all Christians expected to follow their example? Discuss the reasons for your answer to this question.

5. It seems that the Philippian jailer's decision to accept Christ applied not only to himself, but also to all those in his household. Do you believe that his wife, children and slaves could all be saved through a group decision rather than by each one making an individual decision?

Notes

1. Ernst Haenchen, *The Acts of the Apostles: A Commentary* (Philadelphia, Pa.: The Westminster Press, 1971), p. 486.

2. Ibid., p. 487

3. These hypotheses are compiled by Ernst Haenchen, ibid., pp. 489-490.

4. David W. J. Gill, "Acts and the Urban Elites," *The Book of Acts in Its Graeco-Roman Setting*, ed. David W. J. Gill and Conrad Gempf (Grand Rapids: William B. Eerdmans Publishing Company, 1994), pp. 114-115.

5. See Bradley Blue, "Acts and the House Church," ibid., pp. 184-185.

6. See F. F. Bruce, *Paul: Apostle of the Heart Set Free* (Grand Rapids: William B. Eerdmans Publishing Company, 1977), p. 221.

7. C. Peter Wagner, "The Philosophy of Prayer for World Evangelization Adopted by the A.D. 2000 United Prayer Track" (A.D. 2000 United Prayer Track, 215 N. Marengo Avenue, No. 151, Pasadena, CA 91101, 1994), p. 6.

8. See Lester Sumrall, "Deliverance: Setting the Captives Free," *World Harvest* (July/August 1986): 7.

9. *Random House Webster's College Dictionary* (New York: Random House, 1992), p. 1342.

10. Simon J. Kistemaker, *Exposition of the Acts of the Apostles* (Grand Rapids: Baker Book House, 1990), p. 594.

11. R. C. H. Lenski, *The Interpretation of the Acts of the Apostles* (Minneapolis: Augsburg Publishing House, 1934), p. 662.

12. Everett Ferguson, *Backgrounds of Early Christianity*, 2nd ed. (Grand Rapids: William B. Eerdmans Publishing Company, 1987; revised edition, 1993), p. 200.

13. Ibid., pp. 168-169.

14. Martin Luther (1483-1546), "A Mighty Fortress Is Our God." Public domain.

You Win Some and You Lose Some

When Paul, Silas and Timothy were in Troas, God gave Paul a vision in which a Macedonian man said to him, **Come over to Macedonia and help us** (Acts 16:9). The next thing we know they have planted a church in Philippi, which indeed was one of the great cities of Macedonia. But Philippi was not the capital; Thessalonica was the capital of Macedonia.

Passing Through Amphipolis and Apollonia

17:1. Now when they had passed through Amphipolis and Apollonia, they came to Thessalonica, where there was a synagogue of the Jews.

The missionary team had been called to evangelize Macedonia, but after leaving Philippi, they passed through two significant Macedonian cities—Amphipolis and Apollonia—without stopping. Amphipolis was located 33 miles from Philippi and Apollonia 27 miles farther down the same road. When they arrived in each of those cities, they in all probability found lodging at the local inn and spent at least one night in each, but then they pushed on.

Some might wonder why they did not stop to evangelize and plant churches in Amphipolis and Apollonia. Paul's assignment as the apostle to the uncircumcision was to multiply Gentile churches, and these cities were, of course, full of unsaved Gentiles. It would seem logical to plant at least one church in every city they visited. But they didn't. This is not to say they might not have witnessed to some fellow travelers staying with them at the inn, or to people they might have met in the marketplace. But casual witnessing is a far cry from settling down to evangelize.

A plausible way of understanding this is to assume that Paul, Silas and Timothy were adhering to a sound principle of missiology called today "resistance-receptivity theory," or "the harvest principle."

The Harvest Principle

Jesus established the foundation of the harvest principle when He sent His 12 disciples out on their own for the first time. Just prior to that He said, "The harvest truly is plentiful, but the laborers are few. Therefore pray the Lord of the harvest to send out laborers into His harvest" (Matt. 9:37,38).

Every farmer knows that harvesttime is the part of the annual agricultural cycle when the maximum number of laborers are needed. Because the number of available harvesters is invariably limited, they must be deployed as wisely as possible. Farmers know this and make sure their laborers are in fields where the harvest is ripe, not in green fields that have yet to ripen. That, obviously, would be a waste of their time.

Jesus used this analogy for evangelism. Just as different farm crops ripen at different times, so also different populations ripen for the gospel at different times. Missionaries, to the extent possible, should make sure they are present in ripened harvest fields. The bulk of evangelistic work should be done among receptive peoples. It is true that all peoples, whether receptive or resistant, need to receive a witness of Christ, but the greater investment of time, energy and money should be expended among the receptive.

When the 12 disciples went out, Jesus gave them amazingly specific instructions about their evangelistic targets. Three broadly defined people groups occupied the general area in those days: Jews, Gentiles and Samaritans. Jesus said, "Do not go into the way of the Gentiles, and do not enter a city of the Samaritans. But go rather to the lost sheep of the house of Israel" (10:5,6). Both Gentiles and Samaritans were lost and needed to be saved. Jesus came and would die on the cross for Gentiles and Samaritans. But at that time they were not a ripened harvest field. The disciples would have wasted their time trying to reach them. Both groups later became receptive, and great harvests were reaped among them. But not earlier. The disciples on Jesus' mission were to evangelize only Jews—the lost sheep of the house of Israel.

But not all the Jews would be receptive either. Jesus told the disciples how to handle that situation as well. He said, "When you go into a household, greet it. If the household is worthy, let your peace come upon it" (vv. 12,13). This would describe the *receptive* Jews. And the *resistant?* "And whoever will not receive you nor hear your words, when you depart from that house or city, shake off the dust from your feet" (v. 14). Shaking off the dust was a public statement that they did not plan to return. Instead of returning to the resistant, they should rather push out to new frontiers and find those who are receptive—the ripened harvest fields.

How do harvests get ripe? Whether in agriculture or in evangelizing the lost, God is the only one who ripens the harvest. No human being ever manufactured a cauliflower or a persimmon or an ear of corn. Likewise, only the Holy Spirit prepares hearts to receive the gospel message. Paul said, "I planted, Apollos watered, but God gave the increase" (1 Cor. 3:6).

The harvest principle says, then, that good missionary strategy will be influenced by accurately perceiving the moving of the Holy Spirit upon unreached peoples as He is preparing them for hearing and accepting the message of salvation. Paul, Silas and Timothy were implementing that principle when they passed through Amphipolis and Apollonia without attempting to plant a church.

Why Thessalonica Was Ripe

Thessalonica was riper for the gospel than either Amphipolis or Apollonia because it had a synagogue of the Jews. The missionaries' goal was to make Gentile disciples and, oddly enough, the most likely place to see that happen was in the synagogue. I say "oddly enough" because in our day one of the *last* places we would expect to make Gentile disciples would be in a synagogue. As I explained in considerable detail in the last chapter, the major reason for this was that the most receptive people group in the cities of the Roman Empire was the Gentile God-fearers, and the place to find them and share with them was in the Jewish synagogue. This is exactly what Paul did.

....

17:2. Then Paul, as his custom was, went in to them, and

> for three Sabbaths reasoned with them from the
> Scriptures, 3. explaining and demonstrating that the
> Christ had to suffer and rise again from the dead, and say-
> ing, "This Jesus whom I preach to you is the Christ."

We shouldn't jump to the conclusion that Paul preached in the synagogue on the first three Sabbaths he was in Thessalonica. He left soon after preaching on the third Sabbath, so that would have put him in Thessalonica for only about a month. But it appears he was there longer than that. Let me explain.

When Paul later writes to the believers in Thessalonica, he reminisces about what had happened at that time. Among other things, he says, "For you remember, brethren, our labor and toil; for laboring night and day, that we might not be a burden to any of you, we preached to you the gospel of God" (1 Thess. 2:9). Paul and his friends had jobs, perhaps making tents, for apparently some period of time. Offhand, this sounds like more than a three-week visit.

Furthermore, we discover from the letter Paul later writes to the church in Philippi, "Now you Philippians know also that in the beginning of the gospel, when I departed from Macedonia, no church shared with me concerning giving and receiving but you only. For even in Thessalonica you sent aid once and again for my necessities" (Phil. 4:15,16). Two monetary gifts arrive from Philippi, perhaps largely from Luke and Lydia, while Paul is in Thessalonica, and this also appears to cover more than a period of three weeks.

While Paul was in Thessalonica, he was undoubtedly establishing many valuable contacts, building personal relationship, and gaining credibility on which to launch his ministry in the synagogue itself.

The Church in Jason's House

....

17:4. And some of them were persuaded; and a great
multitude of the devout Greeks, and not a few of the
leading women, joined Paul and Silas.

....

A bit more detail of Paul's ministry in Thessalonica is provided
in 1 Thessalonians 1:5: "For our gospel did not come to you in
word only, but also in power, and in the Holy Spirit and in much
assurance, as you know what kind of men we were among you for
your sake." Notice the balance here, which ought to be a pattern
for missionaries today as well. Paul, Silas and Timothy shared
their faith:

• *In word.* **For three Sabbaths [they] reasoned with them
from the Scriptures, explaining...that the Christ had to suffer
and rise again from the dead** (Acts 17:2,3). This was sound doctrinal preaching from the Old Testament, showing how it pointed to Jesus as the Messiah.

• *In power.* Not only were they **explaining** about Christ, but
they were also **demonstrating** the truth. This once again is ministry in both word and deed, characteristic of the models we have
found throughout the Acts of the Apostles. The power ministries
of healing, deliverance, miracles, prophecies and spiritual warfare
undoubtedly were fully active in Thessalonica, although by now
they had become so much a part of the missionaries' routine that
Luke does not find it necessary to mention them specifically.

• *In the Holy Spirit.* The missionaries' ministry was not of the
flesh, but of the Spirit. It was characterized both by the *fruit* of
the Spirit and by the *gifts* of the Spirit. Through the Holy Spirit,
they were in close touch with the Father, and, therefore, they
also could minister.

• *In much assurance.* They could be bold because they knew they were exactly where God wanted them to be and they were obeying God's orders. Paul ministered with deep conviction.

The net result of their ministry was not a mere trickle of converts, but **a great multitude.** Here in Thessalonica, the converts appear to be mostly Gentiles, including **the devout Greeks,** who would have been the God-fearers, and also **not a few of the leading women** (v. 4). These were undoubtedly upper-class women similar to Lydia, possibly including some government functionaries. Paul had an outstanding nucleus for one of the most significant churches he and his group would plant. Further affirming that they were largely Gentiles, Paul later writes that they had "turned to God from idols to serve the living and true God" (1 Thess. 1:9). Jewish conversion would not have involved turning from idols.

This church, like all the others Paul planted, began as one house church, in all probability meeting in the house of a man named Jason (see Acts 17:5). Jason is a Greek name, so he was more than likely one of the God-fearers who heard Paul preach for three Sabbaths in the synagogue. Probably not long after Paul left, the number of house churches in Thessalonica began to multiply, spreading out from their base in Jason's house. The Thessalonian believers were aggressively evangelistic because Paul writes to them a few months later, saying, "For from you the word of the Lord has sounded forth, not only in Macedonia and Achaia, but also in every place" (1 Thess. 1:8).

Driven Out by Angry Jewish Leaders

17:5. But the Jews who were not persuaded, becoming envious, took some of the evil men from the marketplace, and gathering a mob, set all the city in an uproar

and attacked the house of Jason, and sought to
bring them out to the people.
6. But when they did not find them, they dragged
Jason and some brethren to the rulers of the city,
crying out, "These who have turned the world
upside down have come here too.
7. Jason has harbored them, and these are all
acting contrary to the decrees of Caesar, saying
there is another king—Jesus."
8. And they troubled the crowd and the rulers of the
city when they heard these things.
9. So when they had taken security from Jason and the
rest, they let them go.

The persecution of the believers began with the unconverted
Jews. From what we can surmise, proportionately fewer Jews were
present in the nucleus of the Thessalonian church than in some
others. The Jews were envious, just as they were said to be in
Antioch of Pisidia where Paul had planted one of his very first
churches: **When the Jews saw the multitudes, they were filled
with envy** (13:45). Here in Thessalonica, the Jewish leaders may
have been envious for at least four reasons:

1. The Gentile God-fearers were leaving their synagogue to
follow another Jewish leader—Paul.

2. The power of God in miracles and wonders was being manifested through Paul, and not through them.

3. Paul was not requiring circumcision for Gentiles to become
saved, as the rabbis had been advocating through the years.

4. Paul declared, **"This Jesus whom I preach to you is the
Christ"** (17:3). "The Christ" means the Messiah, and the rabbis in the synagogue were supposed to be the first to know when

the real Jewish Messiah arrived. Worse yet, when Paul declared that Jesus was the Messiah, the Jewish leaders came under a cloud of guilt because they, by identification, were to blame for killing Him. Paul mentions this in 1 Thessalonians, where he says the Jews "killed both the Lord Jesus and their own prophets" (2:15). If nothing else, this accusation alone could have incited the Jewish leaders to riot.

The charge against the missionaries, "**Those who have turned the world upside down**" (Acts 17:6), is not a backdoor commendation for effective evangelism, as many might think. F. F. Bruce suggests it is much more serious than that. "The words imply subversive or seditious activity."[1] It was an ominous political charge, implying that the missionaries would advocate dethroning Caesar and installing a rival emperor. It was similar to the false accusation frequently leveled against many American missionaries today, me included, that we are secret CIA agents.

Although the missionaries were not found guilty, they, nevertheless, chose the more prudent action:

> **10. Then the brethren immediately sent Paul and Silas away by night to Berea....**

The Fair-Minded Bereans

> **10. ...When they arrived, they went into the synagogue of the Jews.**
> **11. These were more fair-minded than those in Thessalonica, in that they received the word with all readiness, and searched the Scriptures daily to find out whether these things were so.**

Berea was about 40 miles southwest of Thessalonica. It was not a prominent city, as were Thessalonica or Philippi, but rather an out-of-the-way town. This may be why we have no later Epistle written by Paul to the church in Berea.

Luke mentions that only Paul and Silas left Thessalonica, so perhaps Timothy had remained behind. If he did, he would have joined them later because he is mentioned being with them in Berea in verse 14.

The major reason they would have chosen Berea as their next evangelistic target would, again, have been because of the Jewish synagogue there and the receptive people they would likely find in it. Some say Paul's missionary strategy was to target cities of great social, political and economic significance. This holds true only partially. Berea was no such city. More important to Paul than locating a city of great prestige was the presence of a Jewish synagogue, based on what I have described as the missiological principle of the harvest. That is where he likely would get the most converts.

How long did the missionaries stay in Berea? We do not know exactly, but the chronology seems to indicate that it was probably for several months.

They had a much better time in the Berean synagogue than they did in Thessalonica. They were treated well, and even the Jews seemed receptive to the gospel of Christ. Luke says they were **more fair-minded** (v. 11). Why should this be? Perhaps because Berea was a smaller city and more laid back. It might not have had as much civic pride.

Was the Strong One Bound?

Also, the phrase **that they received the word with all readiness** (v. 11) seems to indicate that the spiritual atmosphere was a bit different in Berea. Somehow the forces of darkness that operate to blind the minds of those who do not believe (see 2 Cor. 4:3,4) did not seem to be as powerful here. Certainly nothing compared to what Paul would soon find in Athens. Knowing what we now know about the power of targeted intercession, it could have been that prayer warriors recruited in Philippi and Thessalonica were on the job and they had done some successful spiritual warfare against whatever territorial spirits might have been assigned to Berea.

To carry this one step further, it could have been that two of the women from the Philippian church, Euodia and Syntyche, had come along with the missionaries as intercessors. Paul says in his letter written later to the Philippians that these two women "labored with me in the gospel" (Phil. 4:3). Their role was much more significant than many commentators recognize. F. F. Bruce, for example, says that a very strong Greek verb is used here and, "Whatever form these two women's collaboration with Paul in his gospel ministry may have taken, it was not confined to making tea for him and his circle—or whatever the first-century counterpart to that activity was."[2]

The verb *synathleo* means "contended" or "strived" or "fought at my side." D. Edmond Hiebert suggests that this verb "pictures these women as having served as Paul's fellow soldiers in the battle."[3] F. W. Beare puts these courageous women right on the frontlines of strategic-level spiritual warfare when he argues that Euodia and Syntyche were "pitted along with Paul 'against principalities and powers...against the spiritual hosts of wickedness in the heavenly places' of Ephesians 6:12, who employ the human opponents of the gospel as their tools."[4] I would prefer to translate Paul's statement in Philippians 4:3 that these women were "doing spiritual warfare on my behalf."

Clarifying the possible role of Euodia and Syntyche does not prove, of course, that they were necessarily here in Berea with

Paul and Silas. Their prayers at a distance from their homes in Philippi could also have been effective in pushing back the darkness from Berea. Nevertheless, on-site praying is to be preferred when it can be arranged. A trend in world Christianity traced to Lausanne II in Manila in 1989, where it first occurred on a prominent level, is to recruit teams of experienced intercessors to pray 24 hours a day through what appear to be milestone events in the advance of the kingdom of God. All of the events associated with the A.D. 2000 United Prayer Track and the Spiritual Warfare Network, for example, are covered by on-site intercessory teams coordinated by Bobbye Byerly, the United Prayer Track prayer leader.

The role of personal intercessors, such as Euodia and Syntyche, in opening the way in the invisible world for the powerful working of God through ministries here in the visible world has been all but neglected in past decades. In my book *Prayer Shield* (Regal Books), I look into reasons for this and also report how things have changed radically in the decade of the 1990s. Pastors, missionaries and Christian leaders of all kinds are now enjoying much more blessing in their ministries by having personal intercessors doing spiritual warfare on their behalf, as Euodia and Syntyche were doing for Paul and his team.

The Berean Church

One of the characteristics of the Bereans was that **they searched the Scriptures daily to find out whether these things were so** (Acts 17:11). The tone of this wording suggests that the Bereans' desire, as they read the Old Testament, was to go into more depth on the matters Paul was addressing, not having any intention of refuting Paul or engaging in polemics. Paul was probably bringing to their attention Scripture passages to which they had not previously paid much attention. It appears that the rabbis in

Berea were as willing to learn from the missionaries as were the common people. This humble desire to hear what God is saying is so commendable that even today Christians like to use the name "Berean Church" or "Berean Sunday School Class" or "Berean Bible School."

In contrast to Thessalonica, a higher percentage of Jews than usual probably participated in the nucleus of this new church. Nevertheless, Gentiles, beginning with the God-fearers, were undoubtedly the majority, as they were in the other churches Paul planted. Interestingly, in Thessalonica Luke makes a point of mentioning that **not a few of the leading women joined Paul and Silas (v. 4)**, and here in Berea he also indicates that among the converts were **prominent women as well as men (v. 12)**. From the first century until now, no matter where we go in the world, the backbone of Christian churches is women. For whatever reason, it is axiomatic that more women than men are willing to give their hearts to Jesus Christ and serve Him with their lives.

More Trouble from Hostile Jewish Leaders

13. But when the Jews from Thessalonica learned that the word of God was preached by Paul at Berea, they came there also and stirred up the crowds.
14. Then immediately the brethren sent Paul away, to go to the sea; but both Silas and Timothy remained there.

The fair-minded Jews in Berea had no problem with Paul and his ministry until hostile Jews from Thessalonica arrived on the scene to stir up trouble. They must have arrived with considerable force. They began looking for Paul, possibly having a warrant for his execution. Paul had known them all too well in Thessalonica, and he wanted nothing more to do with them. His friends helped him slip away under cover of darkness and catch a ship that was heading south on the Aegean Sea toward Athens. Perhaps because of the hasty escape, Silas and Timothy had no time to pack up and go along with him, so they stayed behind in Berea.

Athens: A Stronghold of Darkness

What a contrast between Berea—where people welcomed the missionaries, treated them well, searched the Scriptures, received the word of God, were born again and established a strong church—and Athens, Greece, in all probability the most impenetrable stronghold of darkness of all the cities Paul set out to evangelize! The city of Athens was so permeated with idolatry that the great apostle Paul came and went with minimal results. After the harvests in Philippi, Thessalonica and Berea, Athens must have been an exceedingly depressing experience. From what we know about Paul, he would have preferred any day to be driven out of town by angry opponents of the gospel rather than to be mocked and laughed at and effectively neutralized by sophisticated intellectuals.

From the viewpoint of evangelistic fruit, Athens will not play on Paul's highlight films. For many of us, however, it could have the redeeming feature of serving as a consolation. Many of us have also experienced meager or negative responses to good preaching, just as Paul did in Athens. If it could happen to Paul, there is no reason to think it couldn't happen to us from time to time also. Beyond that, Paul learned some important lessons related to engaging the enemy in Athens, and we can learn them as well.

A City Given to Idols

··

16. Now while Paul waited for them at Athens, his

> spirit was provoked within him when he saw that the
> city was given over to idols.

This is the only place in the New Testament where we find the Greek word *kateidolos*, translated **given over to idols**. Descriptions of the idolatry of Athens abound in ancient literature. It was said that in Athens it was easier to find a god than a human being. Athens was called a forest of idols. Some streets were so full of idols that pedestrians had difficulty getting through. One estimate reveals that more images were located in the city of Athens than in all the rest of Greece combined. The nearest thing I have found that might fit such a description today is Kyoto, Japan, but first-century Athens sounds worse. No wonder Paul **was provoked within him**!

If cities can be said to have personalities, Athens would have boasted an extremely high IQ. For hundreds of years, Athens had been considered by many to be the intellectual center not only of Greece, but also of the whole world. It was the birthplace of the subsequent dominant philosophical tradition of the West. Where did this brilliance originate? It certainly came largely from the forces of darkness over the city. Some might reflect that the knowledge was produced by human minds made in the image of God. This may be true, but the perverse *fruit* of those minds in Athens was anything but. James describes it as "wisdom [that] does not descend from above, but is earthly, sensual, demonic" (Jas. 3:15).

The idols in Athens were the visible front of the invisible spiritual forces that were actively shaping art, philosophy, education and daily life in the city. Not only that, but this influence also strongly radiated from Athens through the whole Roman Empire. The dominant culture was called "Hellenistic (or Greek) culture." Greek was the primary trade language in that part of the world, so much so that the entire New Testament was written in Greek, but mostly by Jews.

Spiritual darkness over a city such as Athens is not something that just happens by a sort of unlucky roll of some cosmic dice. It is rooted in conscious decisions made by human beings. The population of Athens as a whole had voluntarily pledged allegiance to a variety of principalities of darkness, many of which can be identified by name.

For a starter, the name "Athens" was taken in honor of the goddess Athena (also called "Minerva" in Latin). Most cities in the ancient world had chosen to subject themselves and their fate to a so-called "patron deity" or deities. They are what we today would call the territorial spirits. Athena was the "Virgin goddess of wisdom, fine and skilled arts."⁵ Thus, some of her functional names would have been "spirit of wisdom" and "spirit of art." Under her influence, Athens became both the intellectual center and the cultural center of the world. Interestingly, the official seal of the State of California features this same demonic being, and much of what has been recently happening in the state must please her immensely.

Possibly Athena, like the Virgin Mary in Latin America, was another of the disguises of the powerful Queen of Heaven. She exercises such malignant power that even God is repelled by people who choose to serve her. Concerning those who sacrifice to the Queen of Heaven, the Lord says, "Therefore do not pray for this people, nor lift up a cry or prayer for them, nor make intercession to Me; for I will not hear you" (Jer. 7:16). This perhaps could explain why the prayers of intercessors such as Euodia and Syntyche, which apparently were effective in Berea, might have fallen on deaf ears in Athens.

Honoring Demonic Forces Through Festivals

The social life of Athens revolved around periodic celebrations—usually annual festivals—in honor of the multiple deities the people served. Of the scores of such events, eight of them stand out as being the most prominent:

1. *The Festival to Athena herself* (Minerva in Latin). This was called the Panathenaia and was dedicated to what was likely the major territorial spirit over the city. It was held each summer.

2. *The Festival to Apollo* (who used the same name in Latin). Apollo was the spirit of machismo, of male beauty, of what would be epitomized today in the bodybuilding industry. His celebration, also in the summer, was called "The Great Sacrifice."

3. *and 4. The Festivals to Demeter* (Ceres in Latin). Demeter is Mother Earth, a spirit of fertility and likely a spirit of feminism, perhaps countering Apollo's spirit of machismo. In early fall, the Eleusinian Mysteries were dedicated to her honor at the time grain was planted. Later in the fall, Demeter was invited to preside over the Thesmophoria, a fertility festival for women only.

5. *The Festival to Poseidon* (Neptune in Latin). Poseidon was served as the spirit of the sea and the spirit of earthquakes in midwinter.

6. *The Festival to the Dead called Anthesterion.* This was a feast of flowers in early spring, honoring the spirit of death.

7. *The Festival of Dionysus* (Bacchus in Latin). This was a drunken orgy in late spring, dedicated to the spirit of the wine harvest.

8. *The Festival to Zeus* (Jupiter in Latin). Zeus was the high-

est of the principalities of the enemy, known also as the
spirit of the sky and the spirit of weather. His ritual came
at the beginning of each summer.

Each of these, and other festivals, were public displays of worship and sacrifice to these demonic beings. They seemed to be
sending an engraved invitation to the demons to come and do
their things for another year. They usually included the sacrifice
itself, athletic and artistic contests, a procession of great
pageantry through the streets and mystery rites open only to
those few duly initiated into their secrets.

What was the real purpose of these festivals? Everett Ferguson
says, "The festivals are dramatic testimony of the mutual inter-
penetration of religion and all phases of life in pagan antiquity."[6]
The implication of this penetration into all phases of life under-
scores the challenge of separating the wholesome parts of a culture from those that outrightly serve the demonic. No wonder
Paul calls Satan "the god of this age" (2 Cor. 4:4).

Serving the Devil from Morning to Night

The common people of Athens served the demonic spirits day in
and day out. Each family had an altar to Zeus in the yard to protect the home; a pillar dedicated to Apollo to protect the family
members; and a nonpoisonous snake in the pantry, representing
Zeus, which ate the food offered to it each day. At every meal,
they also offered food to Hestia, the spirit of the hearth, and they
had a household altar on which they offered wine to Agathos
Daimon, the "good demon." Good demon? Only those thoroughly deceived by the enemy could believe in any such thing, as
some today tragically think certain kinds of witchcraft may be
good for them.

Throughout the whole countryside, objects created by God

would be used by the Athenians to give honor to a particular evil spirit: mountains, trees, rivers and winds.

The famous philosophers also attributed their knowledge to spirit beings. For example, Socrates, a native of Athens, prayed to Pan, an outdoor spirit that had the legs and face of a goat: "O beloved Pan and all ye other gods of this place, grant to me that I may be made beautiful in my soul within, and that all external possessions be in harmony with my inner man. May I consider the wise man rich; and may I have such wealth as only the self-restrained man can bear or endure."[7] And Plato, also from Athens, said in his *Laws*: "There is also the priestly class, who, as the law declares, know how to give the gods gifts from men in the form of sacrifices which are acceptable to them, and to ask on our behalf blessings in return from them."[8]

Plato taught that "[a] demon [is] a destiny spirit somewhat like a guardian angel as a companion of man, or of cities as well as individuals."[9] This means that it would be desirable for both humans and cities to be demonized indefinitely. This same desire is reflected in some Native-American Indian cultures in which young men are routinely expected to go through a sweat lodge or other ceremony to receive their lifetime demons. This, likewise, is reflected by New Agers who diligently seek their personal "spirit guide."

No Wonder Paul Was Provoked

Luke may well have been putting it mildly when he wrote that **[Paul's] spirit was provoked within him when he saw that the city was given over to idols** (Acts 17:16). Paul had seen idolatry before, but nothing on the scale he saw in Athens. We must be clear, however, about what exactly was provoking Paul. This will not only help us understand what Paul was up against in Athens, but it will also help us greatly to confront many aspects of the

world in which we live today, especially when we are called upon
to engage in spiritual warfare.

Perhaps there were others, but I can see five things in the situation I have described in Athens that would especially provoke
Paul and that should provoke us when we are up against such
things as well:

1. *Invisible spirits were behind the visible idols.* The objects made
of wood, stone, metal or clay called "idols" would not in themselves upset Paul too much. Later he would write, probably agreeing with something the Corinthians had written to him: "We
know that an idol is nothing in the world" (1 Cor. 8:4). What
would upset Paul more than the literal idol were the demonic spirits of the invisible world. These were frequently attached to visible idols who were succeeding in keeping the minds of the people
who served them blinded to the message of salvation Paul was
bringing to them. Paul's primary focus was not on demons, but on
people. Christ did not die to save demons, but to save people. The
demons were provoking him because they were *obstacles* that had
to be removed for the gospel to get through to the people.

2. *Powerful strongholds were binding the population of Athens.*
Two major kinds of strongholds furnish excuses for the enemy to
accomplish his malicious purposes. Paul later writes, "For the
weapons of our warfare are not carnal but mighty in God for
pulling down strongholds, casting down arguments and every
high thing that exalts itself against the knowledge of God"
(2 Cor. 10:4,5). The first kind of stronghold is "arguments" from
the Greek *logizomai*, referring to human ideas or philosophies or
attitudes or actions. The second is every "high thing" from the
Greek *hypsoma*, referring to cosmic powers or spirits.[10] Athens as
an intellectual center and as a religio-cultural center cluttered
with idols had both of these strongholds firmly entrenched.
These strongholds were effectively keeping the gospel of Christ

from flourishing there, and Paul was understandably upset.

3. *The Athenians were serving the creature rather than the Creator.* In Romans, Paul later puts his thoughts on this in words. He writes that "the wrath of God is revealed" (1:18) when human beings do not recognize the glory of God in His creation. The visible world was created so that "His invisible attributes are clearly seen, being understood by the things that are made" (v. 20). To put it clearly, God gets angry when He finds that people such as those in Athens "changed the glory of the incorruptible God into an image made like corruptible man—and birds and four-footed animals and creeping things" (v. 23). What a clear description of Athens! And God can become so angry at such things that He "gives them up" (see Rom. 1:24,26,28). Had He given up on some of the Athenians?

4. *The sacrifices in the idol ceremonies were being made to demons.* Although it is true, as I have said, that an idol in itself is nothing, it is also true that an idol can serve as a medium through which an evil spirit (which *is* something) can actually harm a person in one way or another. Paul combines the two thoughts in 1 Corinthians 10 when he discusses the reasons for not eating meat in idol temples, or more likely in restaurants attached to them, in Corinth. He says that what the pagans offer to idols "they sacrifice to demons..., and I do not want you to have fellowship with demons" (1 Cor. 10:20). The idol is the visible and the demon is the invisible.

Michael Green, a New Testament scholar, offers a perceptive comment on this issue. He says that in the Early Church, "The more common attitude was...to pour scorn, indeed, on the form idolatry takes, but to take very seriously the demonic forces behind it. The demons were fed by the fat of the sacrifices, which was why it was particularly important for Christians to have nothing to do with the sacrificial system." He reminds us that the demons could be overcome by the power of Christ, and that "The Christian's business, therefore, was to wage total war upon them, relying on the victory of Christ."[11]

To put it another way, the people of Athens, while sacrificing to idols, were literally taking communion with demons and inviting them to continue their destructive control over their lives.

5. *The annual festivals to the high-ranking spirits were designed as occasions to renew and extend agreements previously made with the principalities that ruled the city.* Territorial spirits over cities gain their power only through decisions of human beings. Through the centuries, people groups experiencing collective trauma brought on by war, famine, epidemic, natural disaster or any other cause have often sought supernatural power to relieve their situation. Very few turn to God as they did in Nineveh (see Jon. 3:3-10). Most, because of their fallen human nature, turn rather to other sources of supernatural power, such as demonic principalities, for solutions to their problems.

As George Otis Jr., a missiologist, explains, "The overwhelming majority of peoples down through history have elected to exchange the revelation of God for a lie. Heeding the entreaties of demons, they have chosen in their desperation to enter into *quid pro quo* pacts with the spirit world. In return for a particular deity's consent to resolve their immediate traumas, they have offered up their singular and ongoing allegiance. They have collectively sold their proverbial souls."[12]

Once people, such as those in Athens, make such an agreement with evil spirits, how is this maintained? How is their demonic lease extended generation after generation? It is done principally through festivals and pilgrimages. George Otis Jr. says, "These celebrations are decidedly not the benign, quaint and colorful cultural spectacles they are often made out to be. They are conscious transactions with the spirit world. They are opportunities for contemporary generations to reaffirm the choices and pacts made by their forefathers and ancestors. They are occasions to dust off ancient welcome mats and extend the devil's right to rule over specific peoples and places today."[13]

An interesting example of this occurred in Athens itself in 420 B.C. when a plague threatened to wipe out the city. In the face of this trauma, the people of Athens agreed to invite a spirit of psychic healing named Asclepius to save the city, which he gladly consented to do. I am not aware of the price Asclepius might have exacted for his services, but I am sure it was considerable. A. D. Nock comments, "The rise of Asclepius reflects also a tendency for a religion of emergencies to become prominent as contrasted to a religion of normality."[14] This is a confirmation of Otis's notion of traumas frequently precipitating the demonization of people groups or cities. Knowing this, Paul was deeply provoked by finding that practically the entire population of Athens was in captivity to the evil one.

Paul in the Athens Synagogue

17:17. Therefore he reasoned in the synagogue with the Jews and with the Gentile worshipers,...

As was his custom, Paul went into the Jewish synagogue in Athens to share the gospel. Ordinarily, he would find the people in the synagogue most ready to hear and accept the message of salvation. But this was not the case in Athens. Luke, who tells us of converts as frequently as he can, mentions nothing of either Jews or God-fearers in the synagogue being saved. Why is this? Very few of the commentators I am consulting raise this issue, much less analyze the reasons. They generally believe that Paul's address to the Greek philosophers deserves our primary attention here. Simon Kistemaker, however, does make a brief, but plausible, suggestion concerning Paul's synagogue ministry: "We surmise that the membership in the synagogue in Athens was less than that of the synagogues in Berea and Thessalonica."[15] If this is the case, I would like to suggest three reasons why it might have been true:

1. The thickness of the extraordinary cloud of darkness over Athens may have kept pagans from becoming synagogue God-fearers in any significant numbers. True, Luke mentions **Gentile worshipers** in the synagogue there, but the numbers presumably would be nothing like those in the synagogues in Berea and Thessalonica. Furthermore, the idolatrous environment of the city would not have been particularly hospitable to Jews themselves, and because Athens was not known as a commercial center, relatively few Jews might have lived there.

2. Perhaps the Jews who had chosen to reside in Athens had developed a protective shield of tolerance, and the blatant idolatry of the city might not have bothered them much. This certainly would have characterized them as liberal, rather than orthodox, Jews. This in itself could have been the cause of a struggling synagogue that had little social strength.

3. The constant festivals and pilgrimages that offered their sacrifices to the hosts of wickedness over the city would have served to empower the enemy to the extent that he had gained unusual ability to neutralize Paul's evangelistic efforts, both in the synagogue and in the marketplace.

Whatever the reasons, Paul became frustrated enough so that he did something that was not his usual practice.

Paul in the Athens Marketplace

17. Therefore he reasoned...in the marketplace daily with

> those who happened to be there.

Paul tried Plan B. He did not find the usual ripened harvest field among the God-fearers in the synagogue, so he decided to try going directly to the Gentiles. This had worked once on his first term when he and Barnabas went to Lystra, but there a high-profile healing of a man lame from birth had opened the minds of the Gentiles. In Athens, we know of no such miracle, and approaching the Gentiles directly didn't work.

> 18. Then certain Epicurean and Stoic philosophers encountered him. And some said, "What does this babbler want to say?" Others said, "He seems to be a proclaimer of foreign gods," because he preached to them Jesus and the resurrection.

The Athenians insulted Paul by calling him a babbler, which literally means a "seed picker." John Stott comments, "It would be hard to imagine a less receptive or more scornful audience."[16] It gets worse by verse 32 where, according to various translators, "some mocked" or "some laughed" or "some sneered" or "some scoffed." Eugene Peterson in *The Message* puts it vividly: "Some laughed at him and walked off making jokes."[17]

Paul's Speech on the Areopagus

> 19. And they took him and brought him to the Areopagus, saying, "May we know what this new doctrine is of which you speak?
> 20. For you are bringing some strange things to our ears.

Therefore we want to know what these things mean."
21. For all the Athenians and the foreigners who were
there spent their time in nothing else but either to tell or
to hear some new thing.

Undoubtedly, knowing ahead of time that his audience would be a hostile one, Paul decided to go all the way and address the philosophers who regularly gathered on the Areopagus or "Mars Hill." All kinds of people were there, from the Epicureans who taught that we should eat, drink and be merry to get all the pleasure from life possible, to the Stoics who taught that we should submit ourselves patiently to whatever fate might bring through self-control, not pleasure seeking. Tolerating all such philosophies was regarded as politically correct. As for Paul's ideas, they were simply curious to see what this "seed picker" might have to offer. They literally had nothing better to do.

Paul's central theme in talking to these idolatrous philosophers was the relationship between the visible and the invisible. It was a brilliant example of contextualization, beginning by his reference to their "UNKNOWN GOD" whom, Paul said, "you worship without knowing" (v. 23). This is the invisible Lord God who cannot stand to be represented by things made with human hands such as the forests of idols seen throughout Athens. The Creator never takes the form of the creature.

Paul said of this invisible Creator God: "Him I proclaim to you" (v. 23).

This God "made the world and everything in it" (v. 24). He sustains the world and "gives to all life, breath, and all things" (v. 25). He made all human beings:

26. "And He has made from one blood every

nation of men to dwell on all the face of the earth,
and has determined their preappointed times and the
boundaries of their dwellings,
27. so that they should seek the Lord, in the hope
that they might grope for Him and find Him, though
He is not far from each of us."

God made all people from one blood; He designed a variety of human cultures; He set people in defined territories, and He did all this so that human beings could have fellowship with Him and enjoy Him forever.

Why didn't the Athenians know this God who was so close to them? It was essentially that they had chosen, rather, to worship idols and to submit themselves to creatures such as Apollo, Dionysus or Zeus. By doing so, they were breaking the first two of the Ten Commandments of the invisible true God whom Paul was preaching and to whom no idol could be dedicated.

Paul tries to communicate the futility of their idolatry by dealing with the visible. Here he points out two principal ways the creature is commonly glorified instead of the Creator. He mentions "temples made with hands" (v. 24), and "gold or silver or stone, something shaped by art and man's devising" (v. 29). Although the works of human hands can glorify God, from long before Paul went to Athens until now, many human beings have chosen to use architecture and art to glorify the invisible powers of darkness rather than their rightful Creator. For example, a cursory reading of typical commercial tour packages for many nations of the world would show what I mean. They often feature sightseeing of buildings and works of art specifically and overtly intended to glorify demonic forces in a disproportionate way. This does not please God.

God, instead, is glorified by His creation. "His invisible attributes are clearly seen, being understood by the things that are made" (Rom. 1:20). Despite distortions of creation devised by people such as the Athenians, God has His purpose, a redemptive purpose, in all aspects of creation. Every person, every animal, every tree or stone or mountain, every angel, and every city or culture or people group has been designed by God and formed to display His glory when properly understood.

Paul asserts that God made a variety of cultural groups, which he terms **"every nation of men"** (Acts 17:26), **"that they should seek the Lord"** (v. 27). At that moment, Paul deeply desires that one of those groups, the Athenians, open their hearts to truly seek the Lord. To bring them to a point of decision, Paul drops a verbal bomb and tells them to repent!

....

30. "Truly, these times of ignorance God overlooked, but now commands all men everywhere to repent."

....

Paul was in no mood to invite debate or dialogue. He didn't compromise his message and say, "You are so wise that perhaps we can sit down and learn from each other." He didn't take an attitude of "tolerance." He outrightly told them they needed to turn around and go in the other direction. He was telling them to repent of trying to shape the divine nature into art and architecture through fashioning idols and temples. They should worship the invisible God, not the visible objects fronting for demonic powers.

And Paul told them exactly why they should repent—because the God Paul preached is the judge of the whole world (see v. 31), and **"He has given assurance of this to all by raising Him [Jesus] from the dead"** (v. 31).

The Athenian philosophers had endured Paul until he mentioned the Resurrection. That was enough. Their tolerance had
been stretched to the breaking point.

··

**32. And when they heard of the resurrection of the
dead, some mocked, while others said, "We will hear
you again on this matter."**

··

In other words: "Paul, don't call us, we'll call you!" They were
not about to consider giving their ultimate allegiance to Paul's
"UNKNOWN GOD" (v. 23).

You Win Some and You Lose Some

Was Paul's ministry in Athens successful?

The answer to this question could be yes or it could be no,
depending on our understanding of Paul's goals.

If we understand that his goal was to deliver a speech that was
theologically impeccable and yet skillfully contextualized to the
culture of Greek philosophers, we would say he was successful.
Many students of Paul consider his address on Mars Hill as the
finest of all his recorded speeches.

If we understand his goal as winning an argument with the
sophisticated intellectuals of what could be seen as the Harvard
of the first century, we would say he failed.

And if we understand that more likely his primary goal was to
win people to Christ and plant a strong church in Athens, Paul
definitely was much less than successful. Only two converts are
mentioned by name, **Dionysius the Areopagite**, and a **woman
named Damaris** (v. 34). William Ramsay says, "It would appear
that Paul was disappointed and perhaps disillusioned by his experience in Athens."[18]

Did Paul start a church in Athens? We have no Epistle written to the believers in Athens. Howard Marshall points out, "Whether a church was formed at this stage is doubtful; Paul describes some of his Corinthian converts as the 'first fruits of Achaia'"[19] (1 Cor. 16:15). By the time Paul wrote back to the church he was yet to plant in Corinth, Athens had apparently become a dim memory, and undoubtedly an unpleasant one at that.

What Did Paul Learn?

I believe that Paul's experience in Athens, although far from a success in evangelism and church planting, was, nevertheless, a valuable learning experience for him, and by application for us as well. Paul learned important lessons about (1) the awesome power of the enemy, and (2) missionary methodology.

None of the commentators I have checked raise the question whether the demonic powers behind the idols and the festivals and the sacrifices in Athens could have been strong enough to frustrate Paul's evangelistic intentions in the city. I personally believe they could have been, and probably were, frustrating to Paul. This is reminiscent of Jesus' ministry in His hometown of Nazareth. It is said, "He did not do many mighty works there because of their unbelief" (Matt. 13:58). Neither Jesus nor Paul did anything particularly wrong; they simply encountered powers that, at that particular time, were fortified enough to hold their position and prevent the fullest penetration of the kingdom of God.

This is not intended to exalt demonic forces. Ultimately, as I have said many times, they have been, and will continue to be, overcome "by the blood of the Lamb" (Rev. 12:11). It is intended, however, to remind us of the real world of evangelism out there where Satan is deeply entrenched and determined to resist the gospel for as long as he possibly can.

Methodologically, Paul's ministry in Athens seems to have

been much word and little deed. In Thessalonica, Paul's method was both **explaining** and **demonstrating** (Acts 17:3). A church was planted in Lystra, where there was no synagogue at all and where they worshiped Zeus and Hermes, but this came in the wake of the miraculous healing of a lame man (see 14:8-18). No such miracle is recorded in Athens. Brilliant words, unaccompanied by visible examples of God's power, avail little.

Finally, Paul goes from Athens to Corinth where he has a bit more time to reflect on the methodology he had used. When he arrived in Corinth, he was ready to say, "And my speech and my preaching were not with persuasive words of human wisdom, but in demonstration of the Spirit and of power, that your faith should not be in the wisdom of men but in the power of God" (1 Cor. 2:4,5). As Richard Rackham comments, "At Athens St. Paul tried the wisdom of the world and found it wanting....His disappointment at the failure of the former method to touch the frivolous Athenians no doubt kindled the fire with which he denounces the wisdom of the world in his first epistle to the Corinthians."[20]

Many times, missionaries in our day have perpetuated the kind of ministry Paul used in Athens. We have tended to rationalize the gospel and present Christ to the lost on the weight of logical arguments. Most unbelievers, particularly in the Third World and increasingly in the Western world, are not nearly as concerned about reason and logic as they are about power. They will believe the Word more readily if it is confirmed by the deed. Power ministries accompanying the gospel message of salvation in Christ have been severely underutilized in modern times.

Fortunately, this is changing, particularly now that in the years to come we will see more missionaries sent out by Third World churches than by the traditional Western churches. I recently read an inspiring report from Asian Outreach, a Third World mission agency based in Hong Kong. The word they had been receiving from the Asian people they were evangelizing was: "Western missionaries brought us the *knowledge* of God; now Asian missionaries are bringing us the *power* of God!"

You win some and you lose some. Paul won in Thessalonica and Berea, but lost in Athens. He left Athens disappointed, but he had learned valuable lessons that would help spread the Christian movement then and now.

Reflection Questions

1. In Paul's day, some of the most receptive people to the gospel message were Gentile God-fearers. Try to name some equally receptive groups of people in today's world, including in your own community.

2. Euodia and Syntyche were likely personal intercessors for the apostle Paul. Can you think of anyone in your church who has a similar ministry for your pastor? Anyone outside your church who is called to pray for certain leaders?

3. The demonic forces in Athens were honored through certain holidays, festivals and pilgrimages. Can you think of anything we do today that has a similar function? What part should Christians play in this?

4. How is it that invisible spirit beings relate to visible, lifeless forms such as idols? Can a sacrifice to an idol be a sacrifice to a demon?

5. Paul's speech on Mars Hill is regarded as a brilliant address. Why, then, did very little spiritual fruit come as a result?

Notes

1. F. F. Bruce, *Paul: Apostle of the Heart Set Free* (Grand Rapids: William B. Eerdmans Publishing Company, 1977), p. 225.
2. F. F. Bruce, *The Pauline Circle* (Grand Rapids: William B. Eerdmans Publishing Company, 1985), p. 85.
3. D. Edmond Hiebert, *Personalities Around Paul* (Chicago: Moody Press, 1973), p. 166.
4. F. W. Beare, *A Commentary on the Epistle to the Philippians* (London, England: Adam & Charles Black, 1959), p. 145.
5. Everett Ferguson, *Backgrounds of Early Christianity* (Grand Rapids: William B. Eerdmans Publishing Company, 1987; revised edition, 1993), p. 143.
6. Ibid., p. 151.
7. Ibid., p. 136.
8. Ibid., p. 141.
9. Ibid., p. 185
10. J. Blunck says, "The NT use of *hypsoma* probably reflects astrological ideas, and hence denotes cosmic powers." "Height, Depth, Exalt," *The New International Dictionary of New Testament Theology*, ed. Colin Brown (Grand Rapids: Zondervan Publishing House, 1976), vol. 2, p. 200.
11. Michael Green, *Evangelism in the Early Church* (Grand Rapids: William B. Eerdmans Publishing Company, 1970), p. 131.
12. George Otis Jr., "An Overview of Spiritual Mapping," *Breaking Strongholds in Your City*, ed. C. Peter Wagner (Ventura, Calif.: Regal Books, 1993), p. 40.
13. Ibid., p. 42.
14. Cited by Ferguson, *Backgrounds of Early Christianity*, p. 173.
15. Simon J. Kistemaker, *Exposition of the Acts of the Apostles* (Grand Rapids: Baker Book House, 1990), p. 626.
16. John Stott, *The Spirit, the Church and the World: The Message of Acts* (Downers Grove, Ill.: InterVarsity Press, 1990), p. 284.
17. Eugene H. Peterson, *The Message: The New Testament in Contemporary English* (Colorado Springs: NavPress, 1993), p. 278.
18. William Mitchell Ramsay, *St. Paul the Traveler and the Roman Citizen* (London, England: Hodder & Stoughton, 1925), p. 252.
19. I. Howard Marshall, *The Acts of the Apostles: An Introduction and a*

Commentary (Grand Rapids: William B. Eerdmans Publishing Company, 1980), p. 291.

20. Richard Belward Rackham, *The Acts of the Apostles: An Exposition* (London, England: Methuen & Company, Ltd., 1901), p. 320.

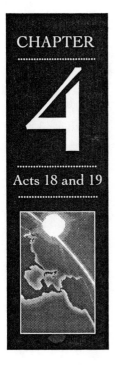

CHAPTER

4

Acts 18 and 19

Corinth
to Antioch
to Ephesus

> 18:1. After these things Paul departed from
> Athens and went to Corinth.

The journey from Athens to Corinth was about 50 miles due west. Both were famous cities in ancient Greece and, therefore, they had many things in common. But as far as Paul's missionary efforts were concerned, the differences were far greater. Here are some of them:

- Athens was a small city and had fewer than 10,000 people, while Corinth was large, having more than 200,000 people.
- Athens was an intellectual and cultural center, while

Corinth was a commercial center that had sea trade to the Ionian Sea on the west and the Aegean Sea on the east.

- In Athens Paul ministered alone (except for a possible short visit by Timothy), but in Corinth he had with him a missionary team.
- In Athens Paul focused on Gentile philosophers, while in Corinth he focused on Gentile God-fearers.
- In Athens Paul displayed brilliance in human wisdom; in Corinth he ministered with displays of supernatural power.
- In Athens the word overshadowed deeds, but in Corinth deeds supported and confirmed the word.
- In Athens he produced little fruit, while evangelistic ministry in Corinth produced a great harvest.

Spiritual Mapping

A further important difference between the two cities of Athens and Corinth was the difference in the apparent depth of demonic entrenchment. Areas or people groups that had not yet been penetrated by the gospel of Christ seemed to have varying degrees of spiritual darkness. George Otis Jr. says, "Regardless of their theology, any honest and moderately traveled Christian will acknowledge that there are certain areas of the world today where spiritual darkness is more pronounced....The question is why? Why are some areas more oppressive, more idolatrous, more spiritually barren than others? Why does darkness seem to linger where it does?"[1]

Answers to these questions, which have been ignored by some and have baffled others, are now becoming clearer through the emerging discipline of spiritual mapping. Even a novice spiritual mapper in the first century would have been able to recognize that darkness lingered over Athens more than over either Berea, Paul's previous stop, or Corinth, Paul's next stop. Luke tells us that in Athens [Paul's] spirit was provoked within him when he saw the city was given over to idols (17:16).

This is not to say that the pagan city of Corinth was without its territorial spirits and other hosts of wickedness that sought to keep its 200,000 people in spiritual captivity. A preliminary attempt to spiritually map Corinth might indicate that at least two territorial spirits had received the allegiance of a great many of its people:

• Poseidon (Neptune in Latin). Poseidon was also worshiped in Athens, but more so here in Corinth. This was the spirit of the sea, a very important deity for the Corinthians to please and to serve because Corinth had two seaports, located as it was on an isthmus. The sea was the source of its considerable wealth. Poseidon would have promised lucrative commerce in exchange for worship and sacrifices.

• Aphrodite (Venus in Latin). Aphrodite was a spirit of free love. Her temple, atop an 1,800-foot hill prominent in the city, was said to have featured 1,000 female slaves who served as temple prostitutes, readily available to all who would glorify Aphrodite and agree to serve her. Few turned her down. Corinth was as well known in ancient Greece for unrestrained immorality as Athens was known for philosophy. Society itself promoted immorality as a virtue. In the Greek of the day, the verb "to corinthianize" was synonymous to "to fornicate."

As a means of accomplishing his purposes of blinding people's minds against hearing the gospel, Satan is said to use the world and the flesh (see Eph. 2:1-3). Poseidon attracted people to the world, while Aphrodite drew them into the flesh. And, although it was not another Athens, Corinth would have had a substantial supply of other demons who served their territorial superiors by deceiving as many individual Corinthians as possible.

Because the Roman proconsul Gallio, whose historic dates are well known, was ruling Corinth at the time Paul was there (see Acts 18:12ff.), we have a fairly certain time span for Paul's ministry in Corinth, arriving in the fall of A.D. 50 and leaving in the spring of A.D. 52.

Paul, the Tentmaker

18:2. And he [Paul] found a certain Jew named Aquila, born in Pontus, who had recently come from Italy with his wife Priscilla (because Claudius had commanded all the Jews to depart from Rome); and he came to them.
3. So, because he was of the same trade, he stayed with them and worked; for by occupation they were tentmakers.

Paul is frequently referred to in missionary circles as a "tentmaker," meaning a bivocational missionary. This implies that the missionaries earn a living by what is usually some sort of secular employment while also doing missionary work in the country or city in which they are employed. Some go as far as to assume that Paul always functioned as a bivocational missionary and, therefore, those of us who desire to follow Paul's example as a missionary should consider doing the same.

Tentmaking is a desirable and necessary option in some missionary work, but in my opinion it should not be seen as an overall principle or as an ideal course to follow. It is true that Paul frequently earned his own living while evangelizing and planting churches. Besides tentmaking here in Corinth, he also did so in Thessalonica (see 1 Thess. 2:9) and in Ephesus (see Acts 20:34), and possibly in other places. He did it sometimes because it was a financial necessity, and it freed him from asking for material support from the new believers. But right here in Corinth, as we shall see shortly, Paul worked less and preached more as soon as money arrived from outside sources. For some reason, it seems that Paul was more reluctant to accept financial support from the Corinthians than from others (see 2 Cor. 12:13), although he had a basic right to accept it (see 1 Cor. 9:6).

In any case, Paul's secular work was always secondary to church planting. This is far different from many contemporary tentmaking missionaries who seldom get around to the arduous task of planting churches because of the competing demands of their secular vocations.

As was customary, Paul settled down in the Jewish quarter when he arrived in Corinth. How he found Aquila and Priscilla we are not told, but one reason he took lodging with them was that as tentmakers they could offer him a job.

Luke doesn't mention it specifically, but historical evidence points to the likelihood that Aquila and Priscilla were already believers before Paul arrived. This derives from Luke's information that they had come from Rome **because Claudius had command-ed all the Jews to depart from Rome** (Acts 18:2). A later statement from a Roman historian, Suetonius, leads many scholars to the same conclusion arrived at by F. F. Bruce: "Suetonius's statement, in fact, points to dissension and disorder within the Jewish community of Rome resulting from the introduction of Christianity into one or more of the synagogues of the city."[2] If this is true, one reason Paul would try to find them is obvious. They were probably charter members of the church in Rome, and they would provide excellent support for new church planting in Corinth.

A Reunion with Silas and Timothy

The last time Paul had seen Silas and Timothy together was when he was fleeing for his life from Berea. He had sent word for them to join him in Athens. Apparently Timothy did come (see 1 Thess. 3:1,2), but he did not have an important enough role for Luke to mention this in Acts. Possibly, evangelizing Athens had not been a part of Paul's strategic design originally. He landed there because it is where the ship on which he had escaped from the infuriated Jews in Berea had been headed, and as it says in Acts 17:16: **Now while Paul waited for them at Athens, his spirit was provoked within him.** Be that as it may, here in Corinth we are told that now **Silas and Timothy had come from Macedonia (18:5).**

By now, undoubtedly many more than three churches were located around Macedonia, but the chief centers of Christian activity would still have been Philippi, Thessalonica and Berea. Presumably, Silas and Timothy had recently been in contact with all three churches when they arrived. They brought with them to Corinth two things Paul greatly welcomed: money and news.

Luke does not tell us here that they brought money, but Paul himself refers to it when he writes to the Corinthian believers three or four years later: "And when I was present with you, and in need, I was a burden to no one, for what I lacked the brethren who came from Macedonia supplied" (2 Cor. 11:9). It must have been a substantial sum of money. Luke and Lydia could have been among the large donors, as well as the **prominent women** (Acts 17:12) mentioned as belonging to the churches in both Thessalonica and Berea, and others.

How substantial was the gift? *The New King James Version,* which I am using almost exclusively, lets us down here. The *New International Version* is more accurate, so I will use it:

> **18:5. When Silas and Timothy came from Macedonia,**
> **Paul devoted himself exclusively to preaching,...**

Because Paul's tentmaking was an option used only when necessary, he was able to give it up and minister full time when the money came from Macedonia. So it must have been a large amount.

Good News from the North

Silas and Timothy also brought good news from the churches up north, especially from Thessalonica (see 1 Thess. 3:6-9). We know this because while Paul was there in Corinth, he wrote both 1 Thessalonians and 2 Thessalonians. It seems strange that Luke does not choose to mention any of the letters Paul wrote. He actually wrote what are now 10 books of the Bible during the span of Acts, but Luke apparently had no idea of the significance Paul's letters would later have throughout history.

Those of us who have served as career missionaries know the joy that comes when we hear news that the churches we have planted are moving forward with the Lord. During the time he was in Athens, something had caused Paul to worry a great deal about the well-being of the Thessalonian believers. He had developed a worst-case scenario in his mind, as he admits in 1 Thessalonians 3:5: "For this reason, when I could no longer endure it, I sent to know your faith, lest by some means the tempter had tempted you, and our labor might be in vain." He had sent Timothy, who was apparently paying him a short visit in Athens, back to Thessalonica to find out what was happening.

Paul's worries were unfounded, much to his joy and encouragement. He writes to them from Corinth: "But now...Timothy has come to us from you, and brought us good news of your faith and love, and that you always have good remembrance of us, greatly desiring to see us, as we also to see you" (v. 6). The three kinds of news missionaries most like to hear were those brought by Timothy:

1. Personal relationships continued strong. Their memories
    of each other were positive, and they wanted to get
    together again as soon as possible.
2. The fruit of the Holy Spirit was being manifested in the
    church. They were characterized by both "faith and
    love."
3. They were spreading the gospel throughout their region.
    "For from you the word of the Lord has sounded forth,
    not only in Macedonia and Achaia, but also in every
    place" (1:8).

To the Jewd First

....

18:4. And he reasoned in the synagogue every
Sabbath, and persuaded both Jews and Greeks.
5. When Silas and Timothy had come from Macedonia,
Paul [devoted himself exclusively to preaching—NIV],
and testified to the Jews that Jesus is the Christ.
6. But when they opposed him and blasphemed, he
shook his garments and said to them, "Your blood be
upon your own heads; I am clean. From now on I
will go to the Gentiles."

....

By now, Paul's evangelistic strategy is highly predictable: He first
goes to the synagogue to preach to the Jews (including both ethnic Jews and proselytes) and the Greeks, who were the Gentile
God-fearers.

For some time, the ministry seemed to go well. The word "persuaded" is from the Greek *peitho*, meaning to win another over
to one's point of view. Paul was gathering converts both from

among the Jews and from among the God-fearers. All seemed to be positive and peaceful.

Then something changed! Serious trouble started in the synagogue shortly after Silas and Timothy had arrived with the money from the churches to the north and Paul then was able to give full time to his evangelistic ministry.

But what was it that changed? It must have been something very controversial, not just the additional amount of time Paul would have had available for preaching between Sabbaths. Apparently what upset the Jews was related to the message that **Jesus is the Christ** or the very Messiah for whom the Jews had been waiting. The theological point behind this that tended to disturb the Jews the most was obviously justification by faith, not by works.

Luke explained this in much detail when Paul did exactly the same thing in the synagogue in Antioch of Pisidia near the beginning of his first term of service. There, **the Jews...were filled with envy; and contradicting and blaspheming, they opposed the things spoken by Paul** (13:45). Here it says they opposed him and were **blaspheming**. What angered them was Paul's message that by faith in Jesus as Messiah **"everyone who believes is justified from all things from which you could not be justified by the law of Moses"** (v. 39). From the Jewish point of view, this would undermine the bedrock on which they had built their theological structure and community, namely obeying the law of Moses as the only way to God. They would immediately understand that one of the implications of **"everyone who believes"** would be that Gentiles can be justified in God's sight and have their sins forgiven without being circumcised and becoming Jews. I can imagine it would be a full-time job for Paul just to sustain the resultant theological dialogue, rabbi to rabbi, with the blaspheming Jewish leaders.

Paul was prepared to put up with such a dialogue for only so long. His goal was not to debate theology, but to evangelize. As time went on, it seems Paul had less and less patience with his fellow Jews. This is demonstrated here first by Paul literally following Jesus' instructions to turn from those who reject the gospel and "shake off the dust from your feet" (Matt. 10:14). Paul **shook his garments** (Acts 18:6), which amounted to the same thing. Second, Paul reminded them of the words of Ezekiel: "When I say to the wicked, 'You shall surely die,' and you give him no warning,...[he] shall die in his iniquity; but his blood I will require at your hand. Yet, if you warn the wicked, and he does not turn from his wickedness, nor from his wicked way, he shall die in his iniquity; but you have delivered your soul" (Ezek. 3:18,19). Such words would not be used either by Ezekiel or by Paul to win friends and influence people. Nevertheless, Paul said, **"Your blood be upon your own heads; I am clean"** (Acts 18:6). Paul's time in the Corinthian synagogue was history!

Also to the Greeks

When Paul later wrote the book of Romans, he said that the gospel "is the power of God to salvation for everyone who believes, for the Jew first and also for the Greek" (1:16). In Corinth, it was now time to go directly to the Greeks.

> **18:7. And he departed from there and entered the house of a certain man named Justus, one who worshiped God, whose house was next door to the synagogue.**

Not only were the Jews eager to get Paul out of their synagogue, but from Paul's own tactical point of view it would also be time to leave. At this point, Paul had gathered a good nucleus of Gentile God-fearers who had been attending the synagogue. His ultimate goal was to build a strong Gentile church in the Gentile city of Corinth, and these new believers could now move out among their unsaved friends and relatives in more aggressive E-1, or monocultural, evangelism. They would be most effective if they could then bring their new converts back to worship in a more familiar Gentile environment instead of into a Jewish synagogue that would have seemed strange and uncomfortable to them.

Paul, therefore, took his fledgling church from the synagogue to Titius Justus's* house, which would be much more "seeker sensitive," as we would say today. Justus was a Roman, and probably a wealthy one at that because his house next to the synagogue must have been a fairly large one. In all probability, he was also called Gaius; it not being unusual for Romans to have three names. We learn that Gaius was one of the few people Paul himself baptized in Corinth (see 1 Cor. 1:14). Also, when Paul returns to Corinth for a visit about six years later, he actually writes the Epistle to the Romans from Gaius's house where he is staying and where the church has been meeting (see Rom. 16:23). Suggesting that Justus and Gaius is the same person helps us understand several pieces of biblical information that otherwise might not be properly connected.

Although the church that met in Justus's house would be composed of predominantly Gentile converts, some believing Jews also formed a part of it. And one of them was a Jewish celebrity:

> **18:8. Then Crispus, the ruler of the synagogue, believed on the Lord with all his household....**

*The first name, Titius, appears in the original Greek and in many Bible versions, but not in our *The New King James Version.*

Crispus's Headline Conversion

When Crispus believed on the Lord, it must have been a headline conversion. I wish Luke had given us more details. Crispus and Justus (Gaius) were two of only three people in Corinth whom Paul baptized personally, all of them presumably VIPs. Was it significant that Crispus had not been converted while Paul was still preaching in the synagogue where Crispus was the president, but he did accept Christ after Paul moved out? We should also take note that this was followed some time later by what was undoubtedly an equally high-profile conversion of Crispus's successor as president of the synagogue, Sosthenes. He is mentioned in Acts 18:1 as being a Jew, but then in 1 Corinthians 1:1 as being a believer.

Answers to questions concerning Crispus's conversion must, of course, be speculative, but in my opinion worth probing at least a bit. Could it be that a demonic spirit of religion had established a strong influence in the synagogue? Could strongholds there have afforded the demon power to tempt Crispus to excessive pride in his authority? Might it be that the domain of that particular spirit was restricted to the synagogue building itself and could not extend to the house next door where Justus lived? If this were the case, the very change in physical location of the church could have loosed Crispus and his family from a spiritual force of darkness over them and allowed him to go next door to hear and understand the glorious gospel of Christ.

Crispus's conversion may have been an illustration of the outworking of a statement Paul makes later when he writes to the Gentile believers in Rome: "For I speak to you Gentiles; inasmuch as I am an apostle to the Gentiles, I magnify my ministry, if by any means I may provoke to jealousy those who are my flesh and save some of them" (Rom. 11:13,14). In Corinth, when Paul moved out and began speaking directly to Gentiles, a prominent fellow Jew and his family were apparently "provoked to jealousy" and then saved.

A further part of the explanation of why Crispus was converted after Paul left the synagogue could also lie in the varied emphases in Paul's ministry. As we have seen many times in Acts, beginning with Antioch of Pisidia, when evangelizing in the synagogues, Paul mostly used the persuasive power of the word—he particularly **testified to the Jews that Jesus is the Christ (18:5).** The message of justification by faith was offensive to the establishment Jews, but it was exactly the good news for which the God-fearers had been waiting, so Paul saw much fruit.

The rest of the Gentiles, however, who did not attend services in the synagogue had not been waiting for such a message. Pagan Gentiles spent much of their lives trying to appease the spirit world, and they were much more concerned about supernatural power than about theological arguments. That is why Paul's major emphasis outside of the synagogue would typically switch to power ministries to prepare people for the message that would follow. None of this is to say that either word or deed would have been absent in either situation, but it is a matter of emphasis. It could well have been that some miraculous event or events Crispus began to witness next door in Justus's house had helped him cross over the line.

Luke's Growth Report

8. ...And many of the Corinthians, hearing, believed and were baptized.

In contrast to Athens, the nucleus of a solid church was formed in Corinth. Both Jews and God-fearers formed the nucleus, but before long it was composed predominantly of formerly pagan Gentiles. They were baptized, but not by Paul. He later said to them, "I thank God that I baptized none of you except Crispus and Gaius, lest anyone should say that I had baptized in my own name. For Christ did not send me to baptize, but to preach the gospel" (1 Cor. 1:14,15,17).

Some of these church members, as in Philippi, Thessalonica and Berea, were from the elite segments of society. This is worth mentioning because some have a tendency to exaggerate Paul's words to the Corinthians "that not many wise according to the flesh, not many mighty, not many noble, are called" (v. 26). Proportionately they may have been few, but they were not absent.

Bradley Blue, for example, suggests that "there were a considerable number of influential home owners who belonged to the Christian community at Corinth."[3] Blue reminds us that house churches were the rule in those days, and that in Corinth believers could have met regularly not only in the house of Titius Justus (Gaius), but also in houses belonging to Priscilla and Aquila, Stephanas (see v. 16) and Crispus. Blue says that these people "personify the type of affluence at Corinth. This is not to say that the majority of the believers were wealthy; however, it clearly indicates that there were congregants who had significant financial means at their disposal."[4]

A Vision at a Crossroads

Paul was at a crossroads in Corinth. As a result of much experience, he knew well the ominous signs of serious persecution. Back in his first missionary term, he had been driven from Antioch of Pisidia and then from Iconium by mobs incited by angry Jews. They finally caught up to him in Lystra and stoned him to death, but God overruled and raised him from the dead.

Earlier in this second term, similar bands of Jews had driven him from Thessalonica and from Berea up north in Macedonia. Now here in Achaia the same pattern was rapidly developing.

Paul's crossroads decision was: Should I leave Corinth or should I stay? Many field missionaries today can immediately identify with Paul's situation. Danger has appeared on the horizon that could result in serious consequences, even death. Some would likely have been suggesting to Paul that the prudent thing for the kingdom of God would be for him to leave while there was still time. He himself must have been praying a good deal, asking God for direction in his precarious situation.

God answered Paul's prayer with a vision. This may seem unusual to many of us today who have been programmed by a Western worldview. Most of us, me included, have never had God communicate to us through a vision. But for large numbers of people in the Third World today, as happened for first-century men and women, receiving a revelation from God through a vision was simply a part of the way life normally was. What did God say to Paul?

18:9. Now the Lord spoke to Paul in the night
by a vision, "Do not be afraid, but speak,
and do not keep silent;
10. for I am with you, and no one will attack you to hurt
you; for I have many people in this city."

Just so Paul would make no mistake, the Lord chose to speak to him eyeball-to-eyeball. He was told not to leave Corinth at that time, but to stay on and (1) he was to keep preaching; (2) the attacks being planned would not hurt him; and (3) there would be much fruit for his ministry in Corinth. Paul, therefore, spent a year and a half in Corinth, longer than he usually stayed in one place. Undoubtedly, one of the reasons God told him to stay in Corinth was that a decision to be made later by the Roman proconsul, Gallio, would have a strong influence on the subsequent spread of the gospel.

Paul's Trial in Gallio's Court

12. When Gallio was proconsul of Achaia, the Jews with one accord rose up against Paul and brought him to the judgment seat,
13. saying, "This fellow persuades men to worship God contrary to the law."
14. And when Paul was about to open his mouth, Gallio said to the Jews, "If it were a matter of wrongdoing or wicked crimes, O Jews, there would be reason why I should bear with you.
15. But if it is a question of words and names and your own law, look to it yourselves; for I do not want to be a judge of such matters." 16. And he drove them from the judgment seat.

No one knows exactly at what point, during Paul's year and a half in Corinth, the trial in Gallio's court actually occurred. After the trial had ended, Luke says that Paul remained a good while (v. 18), so it probably was not toward the very end. In other words, this time when Paul left a city, he left voluntarily according to his own time line, not just a few steps ahead of an angry lynch mob.

The whole Jewish community had become riled. Little wonder! Paul had first used his own credentials as a Jewish rabbi and proceeded to upend their traditional Jewish theology. When he finally left the synagogue, instead of moving across town, he took the nucleus of his Christian church to Justus's house right next door. As if this weren't enough, their leader, Crispus, and his whole family became disciples of Paul. The Jews were by now more than ready to take some radical steps to see if they could get rid of the missionary they now hated.

The Jews' charge against Paul: **"This fellow persuades men to worship God contrary to the law"** (v. 13) is more crucial than it may seem to us at the first reading. Because the Jews knew very well that Gallio would not be concerned with violation of the *Jewish* law, they decided to accuse Paul of breaking the *Roman* law.

Here is the issue. As Bruce Winter points out, "The Jews attempted to force a confrontation between Christians and Roman authorities and did so in relation to the imperial cult."[5] By the time Christianity appeared, the Roman Empire had begun to deify its human emperors, and all Roman citizens were required by law to participate in the festivals and ceremonies that would honor them as gods. Christians, of course, believed in the one true God and, therefore, could not do such a thing. This became a serious problem toward the end of the first century and remained so up to the time of Constantine in the fourth century, as students of church history well know. For more than 200 years, the Roman government was responsible for some of the most indescribable atrocities against Christians ever recorded. But this didn't seem to be a problem as yet in the period covered by the book of Acts. Why not?

Jews, like Christians, also worshiped only one God. The Romans had recognized this, and had declared Judaism a *religio licita*, Latin for a "legal religion." As such, Jews were exempted from the requirements to participate in the imperial cult ceremonies. When Christianity came along, it began as Messianic Judaism and was therefore considered by the Roman authorities as simply a branch of Judaism. For years, at least up to the Council of Jerusalem, many Jews assumed the same thing. But here in Corinth, the Jewish leaders had finally decided to draw the line and declare to the public that Christianity should not be considered a part of Judaism after all. The fact that Christianity was determined to include uncircumcised Gentiles as legitimate members of the family of the true God was something the faithful Jews could not tolerate.

It had occurred to the Jewish leaders that they could deal a crucial blow against Paul in particular and against Christianity in general if they could only get it declared a *religio illicita*, an illegal religion. This would force the Christians to begin to worship the emperor. For this to happen, they would first have to persuade Gallio, the highest Roman authority in Achaia, that Christianity was not, in fact, a part of Judaism. By taking this to Gallio, the Jews were playing for higher stakes than they themselves may have realized.

Gallio's Historic Decision

Gallio threw the case out of court before Paul could take the stand to defend himself. It involved no crime or fraud that had violated Roman law. Gallio could no more understand theological nuances such as Gentile circumcision than many of us today could analyze differences between Sunni and Shiite Muslims. He wasn't interested enough to try to understand it. "The governor ruled it was beyond his legal jurisdiction to try the matter because it was an internal Jewish dispute."[6]

The Jews lost big in Gallio's court. As Bruce Winter says, "They secured the very ruling that no orthodox Jew wanted to hear! Christianity was a sect within Judaism and therefore *religio licita*."[7] F. F. Bruce adds, "It meant that for the next ten or twelve years, until imperial policy toward Christians underwent a complete reversal, the Gospel could be proclaimed in the provinces of the empire without fear of coming into conflict with Roman law."[8]

Adding Injury to Insult

> 17. Then all the Greeks took Sosthenes, the ruler of the synagogue, and beat him before the judgment seat. But Gallio took no notice of these things.

Perhaps by now, Paul and the Christian movement had gained a degree of social acceptance in Corinth and public opinion might have favored Paul. Perhaps some anti-Semitism might have been surfacing as well. For whatever reason, Sosthenes, the Jewish ringleader, was thoroughly beaten. Physical injury was added to the judicial insult, and "Gallio didn't raise a finger. He could not have cared less "[9]

Time for a Second Furlough

In modern missionary jargon, Paul served three terms as a career missionary. When he left Corinth, he had finished two of the terms.

Barnabas was Paul's coworker on the first term when they planted churches in Cyprus, Antioch of Pisidia, Iconium, Lystra and Derbe. On their furlough, they returned to their home base of Antioch of Syria where whatever might have been equivalent to their mission headquarters was located. The most important event of the first furlough was a trip to Jerusalem for the historic Council of Jerusalem. On the second term, Silas, later Timothy, and for a time Luke accompanied Paul. After visiting the young churches, they evangelized in Europe, planting new churches in Philippi, Thessalonica, Berea and Corinth. Paul had also ministered in Athens, and he paid a short visit to Ephesus on his way back to Antioch.

> **18.** Then he [Paul] took leave of the brethren and sailed for Syria, and Priscilla and Aquila were with him. He had his hair cut off at Cenchrea, for he had taken a vow.
> **19.** And he came to Ephesus, and left them there; but he himself entered the synagogue and reasoned with the Jews.
> **20.** When they asked him to stay a longer time with them, he did not consent,
> **21.** but took leave of them, saying, "I must by all means keep this coming feast in Jerusalem; but I will return again to you, God willing." And he sailed from Ephesus.

Silas and Timothy stayed in Corinth, but Paul took Aquila and Priscilla with him. They were to remain in Ephesus while Paul visited Jerusalem and Antioch, and lay the groundwork for his return. The three went to the Jewish quarter of the city to get Aquila and Priscilla settled. Paul had attempted to go to Ephesus two years previously, but the Holy Spirit had turned him around and had sent him rather to Europe (see 16:6-10). Now, apparently, God's timing for evangelizing Ephesus was arriving.

Paul naturally attended the synagogue, and there he came to know the Ephesian Jewish leaders. It seems they had a good relationship because they asked him to stay longer. But Paul wasn't ready for that as yet. The requirements of the vow he had taken gave him a good excuse to leave, but he promised he would soon return.

Paul's Nazirite Vow

What does it mean when it says, [Paul] had his hair cut off at Cenchrea, for he had taken a vow (v. 18)? The so-called Nazirite vow was a recognized Jewish ritual of thanksgiving. Paul was undoubtedly deeply grateful to God for the fruit of his second term of service, and particularly for the large church in Corinth and the legal victory in Gallio's court. Paul's vision that he would not be harmed and that he would have many converts had come true.

We don't know exactly when Paul would have started the period of the vow, but presumably it was sometime after the court case. During the vow, he would let his hair grow and abstain from wine, according to the Nazirite requirements in Numbers 6:1-5. Ordinarily, Paul would have continued to keep the vow until he arrived in Jerusalem and had his hair shaved off at the Temple there (see v. 18), then make an appropriate sacrifice. In Paul's day, however, the Jews had come to recognize the option of ending the vow and cutting off the hair somewhere other than in Jerusalem, but with the proviso that the hair would be delivered to the Temple and a sacrifice made within 30 days.

Why Paul would take that option and have his hair cut in Cenchrea instead of Jerusalem we do not know.

Some might wonder why Paul would take a Nazirite vow in the first place. He may have had several good reasons:

1. We must keep in mind that Paul was still, and always would be, a Jew. He has become such a positive role model for Gentile Christians through the centuries that we are often prone to forget that. As we have just seen, it was important for Paul to maintain the public image that Christianity could legally be regarded as a sect within Judaism. Whenever Paul went to a new city such as Ephesus, he took up residence in the Jewish quarter. Now he was on his way to Jerusalem where many, he knew, had some questions about his Jewishness. A Nazirite vow may have been a visible way to attempt to put these thoughts to rest, and prove to whoever was interested that he was still a good Jew.

2. For Jews, but not particularly for Gentile Christians, the

Nazirite vow was a means of grace, similar to the way many of us view the Lord's Supper. It may have been a time for Paul to reestablish intimacy with the Father.

3. The Nazirite vow may have been a "prophetic act." The advent of the contemporary movement toward strategic-level intercession and spiritual warfare introduces many Christians to prophetic acts for the first time. I define it as follows: *A prophetic act is a visible, physical and public action by an individual or a group, in obedience to the immediate leading of the Holy Spirit, reflecting in the visible world important transactions taking place in the invisible world.*

Biblical examples of prophetic acts include Ezekiel lying on his left side for 390 days, then on his right side for 40 days (see Ezek. 4:4-6), or Joshua piling up rocks in the Jordan River for a memorial (see Josh. 4:7). Contemporary examples of prophetic acts might include Youth With a Mission sending teams of intercessors on the same day for "Cardinal Points praying" to the geographical northernmost, southernmost, easternmost and westernmost points of all six continents; or Pastor Bob Beckett driving two-by-two oak stakes into the ground on the borders of Hemet, California, to raise a prayer canopy over the city.

Fast-Forwarding the Furlough

18:22. And when he [Paul] had landed at Caesarea, and gone up and greeted the church, he went down to Antioch. 23. After he had spent some time there, he departed and went over the region of Galatia and Phrygia in order, strengthening all the disciples.

Undoubtedly, a lot happened during the time period Luke describes in these two verses, but apparently not much that is of interest to him. For Luke, it is a time to fast-forward Paul's travels so he can get back to the important business of evangelism and church planting.

Luke describes Paul's visit to Jerusalem by saying only that **he had landed at Caesarea, and gone up and greeted the church.** In Jerusalem, Paul would have touched base with the elders and he would have burned his hair and made a sacrifice at the Temple to fulfill his Nazirite vow. What else he did we do not know.

Then he would have walked 300 miles north to Antioch, the mission headquarters, staying there for **some time.**

After that, Paul set out over land for Ephesus where Aquila and Priscilla would have by now established their tentmaking business, and prepared the way for church planting.

On the way to Ephesus, Paul again visited the young churches he and Barnabas had planted on their first term in Derbe, Lystra, Iconium and Antioch. We don't know who might have been with Paul. Luke rushes through this time period rapidly as well. Luke's priorities seem to be similar to those of frontier missionaries throughout the ages who are called to reach the unreached, evangelize the unevangelized and win the lost. Typically, missionaries are more interested in:

- Making disciples than in perfecting disciples;
- Evangelizing the lost than in nurturing the saved;
- Pioneer missions than in pastoral care;
- Outreach than in church renewal.

Pointing this out does not at all mean that caring for believers and reviving the church are unimportant. God Himself tells us that these ministries are extremely important, and He calls many members of the Body of Christ to those kinds of ministries. He gives these missionaries the spiritual gifts of pastor, mercy, service, prophecy, teaching, administration, hospitality and many other gifts.

Frontier missionaries such as Paul will not neglect to care for the believers and the churches they are responsible for bringing into the Kingdom. Paul himself visited the churches in Derbe, Lystra, Iconium and Antioch no less than three separate times after he planted them. And Paul's nine Epistles later written to the churches brilliantly display his deep desire for their growth and their maturity in the things of the Lord. But because these Epistles are so prominent in the New Testament, some have concluded that Paul's chief priority must have been Christian nurture. My opinion is that Paul's chief priority never deviated from winning the lost.

By his selective way of compiling history, Luke seems to support the thesis I detailed in chapter 1, arguing that pioneer missionaries must always be on guard against succumbing to the "syndrome of church development."

Apollos's Ministry in Ephesus and Corinth

24. Now a certain Jew named Apollos, born at
Alexandria, an eloquent man and mighty in the
Scriptures, came to Ephesus.
25. This man had been instructed in the way of the Lord;
and being fervent in spirit, he spoke and taught
accurately the things of the Lord, though he
knew only the baptism of John.
26. So he began to speak boldly in the synagogue.
When Aquila and Priscilla heard him, they took him aside
and explained to him the way of God more accurately.
27. And when he desired to cross to Achaia, the
brethren wrote, exhorting the disciples to receive him;
and when he arrived, he greatly helped those who

had believed through grace;
28. for he vigorously refuted the Jews publicly, showing
from the Scriptures that Jesus is the Christ.

....

Apollos is a well-known figure among Christians, although the
only information we have of him is right here as well as several
brief references to him in 1 Corinthians. We do know that he was
a Jew from Alexandria, Egypt. Alexandria was the second-largest
city in the Roman Empire after Rome, and it also had a large
population of Jews. John Drane says, "There were probably more
Jews living in....Alexandria in Egypt than there were in Jerusalem
itself."[10] Apollos was eloquent and well educated and knew the
Old Testament thoroughly. He was a bold debater and an apolo-
gist. He knew much about Jesus, but had received only John the
Baptist's baptism. However, he was also a learner and was willing
to be instructed by Aquila and Priscilla in Ephesus.

Where do all these facts lead us? Mainly to frustration! Hans
Conzelmann says it well, if wistfully: "If we only knew whether
Apollos had become acquainted with Christianity while still at
Alexandria!"[11]

Let's try to construct a reasonable explanation. Christianity in
the form of Messianic Judaism did exist in Alexandria, supposing
that the Hellenistic believers when driven out of Jerusalem went
south to Alexandria as well as north to Antioch. Luke's story of
the Ethiopian eunuch (see Acts 8:26-40) shows one way the
gospel indeed reached Africa. The fact that some missionaries
later went out from North Africa (see 11:20) also indicates that
churches must have been planted there. These believers, however, would have experienced the baptism of Jesus, so apparently
Apollos had not been in touch with them, a viable possibility
because of the huge Jewish population in Alexandria. So in

Alexandria, some groups could well have followed Jesus and other groups followed John.

How did John's disciples get there? Let's suppose some Jews from Alexandria happened to be in Palestine when John the Baptist was actively ministering. Some of them could also have been baptized by John in the Jordan River, learned a good bit about Jesus, then returned to Alexandria. Conybeare and Howson affirm that "Many Jews from other countries received from the Baptist their knowledge of the Messiah, and carried with them this knowledge on their return from Palestine."[12] Apollos could easily have been among the first or second generation of these disciples.

Paul Finds Apollos's Disciples *Acts 19*

As many would know, chapters and verses do not appear in the original manuscripts of the Bible. Most of the chapter divisions we are accustomed to are good, but this particular division between Acts 18 and Acts 19 seems to me to be in the wrong place. The following passage is best understood as a continuation of Acts 18:

19:1. And it happened, while Apollos was at Corinth, that Paul, having passed through the upper regions, came to Ephesus. And finding some disciples

2. he said to them, "Did you receive the Holy Spirit when you believed?" So they said to him, "We have not so much as heard whether there is a Holy Spirit."

3. And he said to them, "Into what then were you baptized?" So they said, "Into John's baptism."

4. Then Paul said, "John indeed baptized with a baptism of repentance, saying to the people that they

should believe on Him who would come after him,
that is, on Christ Jesus."
5. When they heard this, they were baptized
in the name of the Lord Jesus.
6. And when Paul had laid hands on them,
the Holy Spirit came upon them, and they spoke
with tongues and prophesied.
7. Now the men were about twelve in all.

When considered as a continuation of chapter 18, we can see clearly that these 12 were disciples of Apollos. E. M. Blaiklock agrees, saying, "Perhaps they were a remnant of Apollos' less-mature ministry in the city."[13] But were they Christians? The usual way Luke uses the word "disciples" from the Greek *mathetai* means Christians. But could they be real Christians without being baptized in the name of Jesus and without knowing anything about the Holy Spirit?

This is the kind of question many missionaries frequently face. The dividing line between those who are truly in the Kingdom and those on the outside is not always as clear as we would like. How about Jesus' own disciples after being with Him for one year? Were they Christians? They certainly had a great deal more to learn, including accurate knowledge about the Holy Spirit. Whether they were baptized in Jesus' name at that time we do not know.

Nativistic Movements

Groups of believers similar to Apollos's disciples are known by many as "nativistic movements." They usually begin without the influence of informed missionaries or evangelists. For example, years ago a pastor in Venezuela told me he had been traveling through the jungle when he suddenly came across a whole village of Christians. He knew that no preacher had ever gone to the area, but he learned that a young man from the area had taken some goods to the market in the city and had been given a Bible. When he returned, everyone in the village took an interest in this new book, and before long all had given their lives to Christ.

The pastor went on to explain that when he found these people, they had developed only three "heresies": (1) they worshiped on Saturday instead of Sunday; (2) they abstained from eating pork; and (3) they had killed all their dogs because their Bible said, "Beware of dogs" (Phil. 3:2)!

Examples run from this rather humorous incident to more serious ones, such as a committed believer in the house churches in China who, lacking sound instruction, sacrificed his son, desiring to imitate Abraham on Mount Moriah (see Gen. 22:1-14).

An important thing about such folks is that they are more than willing to change what they are doing wrong the minute they receive more accurate teaching, just as Apollos himself and Apollos's disciples did. This openness to the truth is one indication in itself that, although they may not be able to verbalize it, the Holy Spirit to some degree has been present in their lives.

Receiving the Holy Spirit

It is notable that Paul's examination of the orthodoxy of Apollos's disciples begins with a question about the third Person of the Trinity, the Holy Spirit. He then moves on to ask about the second Person, Jesus Christ. In response, they believed in the second Person and were baptized in Jesus' name; then they received the Holy Spirit.

Speaking in tongues was a common way to verify whether the Holy Spirit had come into a person's life. Back in Cornelius's house, **the gift of the Holy Spirit had been poured out on the**

Gentiles also (Acts 10:45). How did they know? **For they heard them speak with tongues and magnify God** (v. 46). This later helped Peter convince the Jewish leaders in Jerusalem that Gentiles could be saved (see 11:17; 15:8).

Some, however, use this as a proof text for a doctrine that born-again Christians (not uninstructed disciples of Apollos) should all expect to receive the Holy Spirit as a second blessing after the first blessing of salvation, and that the invariable initial physical evidence is speaking in tongues. This is usually called "baptism in the Holy Spirit." Others, and I find myself part of this group, believe that Holy Spirit baptism ordinarily takes place as a part of conversion because Paul says, "For by one Spirit we were all baptized into one body" (1 Cor. 12:13). We prefer to call subsequent experiences "fillings of the Holy Spirit."

Whereas these differences of opinion, unfortunately, have become reasons for some serious divisions in the Body of Christ in the recent past, fortunately, currently, the barriers they have created are coming down rapidly. More and more we mutually agree that there may be several legitimate ways of understanding the same biblical evidence. No matter how we choose to interpret stories such as Paul's ministry to Apollos's disciples in Ephesus, on a deeper level we share an honest mutual desire to obey the Scriptures, serve our Lord, receive the maximum fullness of the Holy Spirit and get on with the task of winning our world to Christ. As a result, Christians around the world are more united in heart, mind and spirit than they possibly have been for centuries.

Reflection Questions

1. Paul earned his living in Corinth by making tents. What are the pros and cons of missionaries today holding down jobs as opposed to receiving outside financial support?

2. Paul generally preached first in the synagogue, concentrating on God-fearers, when he evangelized a new city such as Corinth. Why was this seen as good missionary strategy?
3. When persecution became strong in Corinth, God told Paul through a vision to stay on in Corinth. Have you or has anyone you know ever had such a direct personal word from God?
4. Paul's Nazirite vow is seen as a "prophetic act." What is your understanding of a prophetic act? Do we ever see such things today?
5. When Apollos's disciples received the Holy Spirit, they spoke in tongues. Does this always happen? Does it ever happen today? How important is this issue?

Notes
   1. George Otis Jr., "An Overview of Spiritual Mapping," *Breaking Strongholds in Your City*, ed. C. Peter Wagner (Ventura, Calif.: Regal Books, 1993), p. 36.
   2. F. F. Bruce, *The Book of Acts* (Grand Rapids: William B. Eerdmans Publishing Company, 1954; revised edition, 1988), p. 347.
   3. Bradley Blue, "Acts and the House Church," *The Book of Acts in Its Graeco-Roman Setting*, ed. David W. J. Gill and Conrad Gempf (Grand Rapids: William B. Eerdmans Publishing Company, 1994), p. 172.
   4. Ibid., p. 177.
   5. Bruce W. Winter, "Acts and Roman Religion: B. The Imperial Cult," *The Book of Acts in Its Graeco-Roman Setting*, vol. 2, pp. 98-99.
   6. Ibid., p. 100.
   7. Ibid., p. 101.
   8. Bruce, *The Book of Acts*, p. 354.

9. Eugene H. Peterson, *The Message: The New Testament in Contemporary English* (Colorado Springs: NavPress, 1993), p. 330.
10. John W. Drane, *Early Christians* (San Francisco: HarperSanFrancisco, 1982), p. 19.
11. Hans Conzelmann, *History of Primitive Christianity* (Nashville: Abingdon Press, 1973), p. 160.
12. W. J. Conybeare and J. S. Howson, *The Life and Epistles of St. Paul* (London, England: Longmans, Green and Co., 1875), pp. 364-365.
13. E. M. Blaiklock, *Acts: the Birth of the Church* (Grand Rapids: Fleming H. Revell Company, 1980), p. 189.

Invading Diana's Territory

Acts 19 is one of my favorite chapters. Paul's ministry in Ephesus was by just about anyone's measurement the most outstanding success story of his missionary career. E. M. Blaiklock says it well: "Luke introduces what must have been the greatest triumph of Paul's life—the evangelization of the Province of Asia."[1]

As we have seen, Paul had set out to evangelize Asia once before, at the beginning of his second term of service. But at that time, Paul, Silas and Timothy **were forbidden by the Holy Spirit to preach the word in Asia** (16:6). The obvious reason for God closing the door on the first attempt was that the timing could not have been right. Often when we look back on such an incident, we never really know why the timing might or might not have been right. In such cases, we simply trust in the wisdom of a sovereign and omniscient God. But for this time at least, it could be plausible to speculate that Paul himself might not yet have been ready to tackle the formidable spiritual strongholds in Ephesus. At that point, he did not have the maturity, experience and the seasoning he subsequently acquired through:

- Dealing with the Python spirit in Philippi;
- Personally experiencing the virtually impenetrable cloud of spiritual darkness holding Athens in captivity;
- Gallio's decision in Corinth that Christianity was, indeed, a *religio licita*, a legal Roman Empire religion.

In Ephesus, Paul was to enter a spiritual battle of enormous magnitude. In this case (unlike the battle in Athens) he, by the power of God, would win, and, therefore, he would see churches multiplied not only in the city itself, but also throughout the whole province of Asia. It is fitting that we are about to see Paul's greatest victory because this is also the last recorded incident we have of Paul planting new churches.

The City of Ephesus

Ephesus was the third or fourth largest city in the Roman Empire after Rome, Alexandria and possibly Antioch of Syria. Clinton Arnold reports that population estimates "begin at a quarter of a million."[2] Ephesus was a city of elegant architecture. Around A.D. 20, Strabo wrote that "the city, because of its advantageous situation...grows daily, and is the largest emporium in Asia this side of the Taurus."[3] Administratively, Ephesus was a free Greek city within the Roman Empire. It handled its own internal affairs under the jurisdiction of a Roman proconsul.

Ephesus was also a principal center of magic for the ancient world. Bruce Metzger says, "Of all ancient Graeco-Roman cities, Ephesus...was by far the most hospitable to magicians, sorcerers, and charlatans of all sorts."[4] Magic, as many would know, is any process by which human beings become able to manipulate supernatural power for their own ends.

A Fetish Factory

One of the best-known objects used for magic in the ancient world was the "Ephesian writings." F. F. Bruce says, "The phrase 'Ephesian writings' was commonly used in antiquity for documents containing spells and formulae...to be placed in small cylinders or lockets worn around the neck or elsewhere about the person."[5] What Bruce is referring to are what are known throughout animistic cultures, such as in Ephesus, as fetishes.

Such fetishes are much more than just quaint artistic objects that have cultural significance. In many cases, they are vehicles through which powers of the spirit world are given varying degrees of freedom to operate in the natural world. For example, I once prayed for a woman to be healed and had no results until God told me to have her remove the object she wore around her neck. After that the healing took place readily.

On another occasion, a missionary wife in Japan had been suffering headaches and nausea beyond medical diagnosis. When my wife, Doris, and I learned that a standard procedure in the construction of Japanese buildings was to deposit an occult fetish in a strategic place, we thought we might have a clue regarding the circumstances. Not knowing exactly where the fetish might be, we escorted the missionary and her husband through every room in their rented house, breaking the power of any spirits present in each room in the name of Jesus and commanding them to leave the house. The headaches and nausea disappeared. Obviously, the fetish was still present somewhere, but the spiritual power it had attracted was gone.

Ephesus was known as the premier fetish factory of the Roman

Empire. No wonder the silversmiths who manufactured many of them were ready to riot when the spirit world over Ephesus began to be torn apart as a result of the spiritual warfare initiated by the arrival of the apostle Paul!

Three Months in the Synagogue

19:8. And he [Paul] went into the synagogue and spoke boldly for three months, reasoning and persuading concerning the things of the kingdom of God.
9. But when some were hardened and did not believe, but spoke evil of the Way before the multitude, he departed from them and withdrew the disciples,...

Paul naturally had settled down with Aquila and Priscilla in the Jewish quarter of Ephesus, which was known to be a relatively large one. Luke doesn't tell us here that he made his own living, but Paul himself mentions that he did when he later returns to teach the Ephesian pastors (see 20:33-35). Paul had left Aquila and Priscilla in Ephesus on his brief visit on his way from Corinth to Jerusalem (see 18:18), and presumably they had set up their tentmaking business before Paul joined them.

Spending three months in the synagogue and having relatively few problems was longer than usual. This problem-free time could be because Paul had succeeded in establishing good relationships with the leaders on his previous visit. Perhaps also Aquila and Priscilla had become active synagogue members while Paul was on furlough and had thereby continued to nurture those relationships.

Eventually, however, the usual happened and the Jews in the synagogue turned against Paul. In Corinth, they did so because he was preaching that **Jesus is the Christ** (v. 5), and here in Ephesus because he was **reasoning and persuading concerning the things of the kingdom of God** (19:8). Same difference! It again boils down to the issue that faith in Jesus Christ is the only way to salvation, and, therefore, that Gentiles can be saved, as well as Jews, but without being circumcised.

Before the three months had ended, Paul had developed his nucleus of new converts. Luke says he **departed from them [the synagogue] and withdrew the disciples** (v. 9). Disciples, as I have mentioned, should ordinarily be taken as a synonym for Christians.

It is not hard to imagine how upset the Jewish leaders would have been with this blatant case of what some today would call "sheep stealing." But this was Paul's normal pattern. In most cases, the initial growth of the new Christian church came at the expense of the Jewish synagogue. Although the synagogue leaders must have been upset, the eventual outward persecution in Ephesus, unlike what we saw in Thessalonica, Corinth and other places, does not originate with the Jews but with the pagan Gentiles.

Two Years Among the Gentiles

9. ...[Paul] departed from them and withdrew the disciples, reasoning daily in the school of Tyrannus.
10. And this continued for two years, so that all
who dwelt in Asia heard the word of the Lord Jesus,
both Jews and Greeks.

Tyrannus, from the best we can understand, was a local teacher who had his own school facility. The Western text of the Greek New Testament says that Paul taught from the fifth to the tenth hour, or from 11:00 A.M. to 4:00 P.M. every day. Tyrannus would in all probability have been using the school in the mornings. The Ephesians kept a strict siesta. William Ramsay says, "Public life in the Ionian cities ended regularly at the fifth hour [11:00 A.M.]."[6] One historian reportedly commented that more people in Ephesus were asleep at 1:00 P.M. than at 1:00 A.M.!

Leadership Training

This is one of the clearest examples of formalized leadership training we have in the New Testament, apparently something different from the ordinary teaching Paul and the pastors would do in their house churches or from house to house. This appears to be what we now would regard as a form of systematic ministerial training. Paul had established a virtual seminary, which we might a bit playfully call "The Siesta Theological Seminary" because many, if not most, of Paul's disciples would be working people who would be giving up their lunch hours and their siestas to take the training courses.

What would the curriculum have been like in the seminary? Luke seems to suggest a cause-and-effect relationship between The Siesta Theological Seminary and the fact that **all who dwelt in Asia heard the word of the Lord Jesus** (v. 10) before the end of two years. This means that the chief focus of the curriculum was likely to have been evangelism and church planting.

Paul, then, was training and sending out church planters as rapidly as he could. This is not to be seen as a deviation in Paul's ministry from evangelism to Christian nurture. Paul was not hereby falling into the trap of the "syndrome of church development," which I have mentioned from time to time. Pastoral care and the nurture of ordinary believers was also occurring in Ephesus, but that would be taking place in the house churches that would have been multiplying in considerable numbers throughout the city during Paul's two years in Ephesus. Paul's seminary classes might have admitted some of the ordinary believers as well, but his priority would more likely have been to train the pastoral leaders God had selected and to put special emphasis on church planters.

Modern missionaries should take their direction from Paul's example. As I am writing this, more people are becoming Christians worldwide than ever before, in geometrically ascending proportions. With the exception of those called to begin work among the 2,500 yet unreached people groups in today's world, there is no longer a great need for cross-cultural missionaries to do direct evangelism. It is, in fact, being done in most parts of the world much like evangelism was being done in the first century—excited new believers spread their faith wherever they went. Some reports reveal that up to 35,000 people are being saved every day in China alone. The great missionary challenge in China is not so much evangelism as it is leadership selection and training. Many of the new converts will be weak Christians or drawn back into the world without the vigorous multiplication of churches under trained leadership.

By trained leadership, I do not necessarily mean those who have college and seminary degrees. The number of church planters who have such academic credentials is minuscule in proportion to the number of new churches being planted each day around the globe. I mean doing what Paul was apparently doing in Ephesus—taking gifted believers whoever they might be, with whatever education they might have, providing for them the conceptual and practical tools they need, and sending them out to extend the kingdom of God. It paid off then and such a training design will pay off now.

Engaging in Spiritual Warfare

I would imagine that a significant part of the course content in

The Siesta Theological Seminary would also have focused on spiritual warfare. Whatever happened in Paul's ministry while in Ephesus would cause him later to write to the believers with these words: "For we do not wrestle against flesh and blood, but against principalities, against powers, against the rulers of the darkness of this age, against spiritual hosts of wickedness in the heavenly places" (Eph. 6:12). Clinton Arnold has found that the book of Ephesians contains "a substantially higher concentration of power terminology than in any other epistle attributed to Paul."[7]

Some take a passage in 1 Corinthians as an indication that Paul could have been involved in some particularly high-level spiritual warfare while he ministered in Ephesus. Actually, 1 Corinthians was written during the time Paul was still in Ephesus, and in it he remarks: "If, in the manner of men, I have fought with beasts at Ephesus" (15:32). F. F. Bruce says that "in the manner of men" means "figuratively speaking."[8] What, then, does Paul figuratively mean? It could be that "beasts" refers to some human opponents, as many suspect. But it could also mean Paul was engaged in battle with the dark angels of the city in strategic-level spiritual warfare. His language in Ephesians that "we don't wrestle against flesh and blood" would seem to bear out the latter interpretation.

Dealing with the Demonic

In the book of Acts, Luke gives only two examples of Paul's dealing directly with the demonic: the episode with the Python spirit in Philippi and the episode in Ephesus. Does this mean that in Paul's evangelistic and missionary strategy, dealing with the demonic is secondary and sporadic and, therefore, not very important for us today? This is what some who oppose strategic-level spiritual warfare argue. But I do not believe it is a correct conclusion. Luke is characteristically selective about the places he chooses to emphasize one important aspect or another of Paul's ministry. Once doing that, he sees little need to repeat it each time it might have occurred.

The best example of this is Paul's message of justification by faith apart from the Jewish law. Most everyone would agree that this was a crucial part of his message wherever he went. But Luke gives us the details of this only once, in Antioch of Pisidia (see Acts 13:38,39). We assume that Paul also preached justification by faith in Berea, Derbe or Thessalonica, for example, but not because Luke tells us he did. We can conclude, therefore, that the number of times Luke chooses to highlight a particular component of Paul's total ministry is not necessarily an indication of where it might have fit on his priority scale.

I think Michael Green, in his classic work *Evangelism in the Early Church*, has an insight that throws considerable light on this matter. He starts with Paul's testimony that in Thessalonica "our gospel did not come to you in word only, but also in power, and in the Holy Spirit and in much assurance" (1 Thess. 1:5). (We should note that if all we had was Luke's account of this in Acts, these facts would have been hidden from us.)

Green points out that the Greek for "much assurance" is *plerophoria*, which includes two dimensions:

1. Powerful preaching. This is as far as many commentators go.

2. But Green also says, "There was another dimension to this power. It involved healings and exorcisms," which "continued throughout not only the apostolic church but into the second and third centuries, to look no further. Christians went out into the world as exorcizers and healers as well as preachers."[9] From this, we can conclude that power ministries, including dealing directly with the demonic in spiritual warfare, were so much part and parcel of the customary ministry of evangelists and mission-

aries that it would not necessarily merit mention in Acts every time it had occurred.

History According to Ramsay MacMullen

Ramsay MacMullen, a Yale University historian, has developed a reputation as a foremost scholar of the Roman Empire. One of the historical phenomena all Roman Empire specialists are compelled to deal with was the incredibly rapid spread of Christianity, culminating with the conversion of the Emperor Constantine in A.D. 312. Christianity from then on became the dominant religion in the Roman Empire. MacMullen reports his research on this in a remarkable book, *Christianizing the Roman Empire*.

According to MacMullen, the chief factor accounting for the astounding church growth in the first four centuries was power ministries in the form of miracles and healings, but particularly as exhibited by dealing with the demonic. He says, "The manhandling of demons—humiliating them, making them howl, beg for mercy, tell their secrets, and depart in a hurry—served a purpose quite essential to the Christian definition of monotheism: it made physically (or dramatically) visible the superiority of the Christian's patron Power over all others."[10]

Although he doesn't use the term, Ramsay MacMullen has concluded that power encounters on levels higher than individual deliverance played a chief role in the vigorous spread of Christianity. Toward the end of the book, he summarizes his thesis by saying that the principal factors were: "emphasis on miraculous demonstration, head-on challenge of non-Christians to a test of power, *head-on confrontation with supernatural beings inferior to God*, and contemptuous dismissal of merely rational, especially Greek philosophical, paths toward true knowledge of the divine"[11] (emphasis mine). He then refers specifically to what we call strategic-level spiritual warfare by saying: "Where once [the saints and bishops] had driven devils only from poor souls possessed, now they can march into the holiest shrines and, with spectacular effect before large crowds, expel the devils from their very homes."[12]

Ephesus as a Battleground

Acts 19 is the only account of ministry in the Scriptures where we find references to all three levels of spiritual warfare:

1. Ground-level spiritual warfare—vv. 11-18.
2. Occult-level spiritual warfare—v. 19.
3. Strategic-level spiritual warfare—vv. 23-41

As I have mentioned repeatedly, we must always keep in mind that these are not three categories unrelated to each other. Rather, they are vitally interrelated in the spirit world in ways of which we may know nothing. What we do know is that spiritual warfare on any one of the three levels can, and does, have varying degrees of influence on the other two. Susan Garrett, a Yale biblical scholar, makes a careful study of the incident involving the seven sons of Sceva in her excellent book, *The Demise of the Devil*. She argues strongly that the demon's victory over the seven sons of Sceva (which we would see as *ground-level*) was the factor that most contributed to the defeat of magic in Ephesus and the conversion of the magicians (which we would see as *occult-level*).[13] I would add that this, in turn, began the process of shattering the awesome power of Diana of the Ephesians (which we would see as *strategic-level*) without Paul so much as confronting this territorial spirit directly.

Let's now take a closer look at spiritual warfare on all three levels in Ephesus.

Ground-Level Spiritual Warfare

Luke's section on ground-level spiritual warfare, which refers to casting demons out of individuals, comes in two parts. First, Luke tells us how to do it, and second, Luke tells us how *not* to do it.

....

**11. Now God worked unusual miracles
by the hands of Paul,
12. so that even handkerchiefs or aprons were brought
from his body to the sick, and the diseases left them and
the evil spirits went out of them.**

....

I love the way Luke uses the phrase **unusual miracles**. The immediate implication is that if some miracles are *unusual*, then other miracles must be *usual* or *ordinary*. Compared to no miracles at all, any miracle might be regarded as unusual. But in places where the Holy Spirit is moving in a revival atmosphere and where miracles are not uncommon, we do find ourselves even today distinguishing unusual miracles from the ordinary ones.

In recent years, I have spent a good deal of time in Argentina where revival has been spreading for more than 10 years at this writing. Argentine leaders definitely have created categories for various grades of miracles. For example, healings of ulcers, hernias, breast cancers and headaches are usual. Unusual miracles would include a lung that had been surgically removed and had grown back after prayer, obese people losing weight (one woman lost 32 pounds) in healing services, and heads of hair growing out on bald men. Filling teeth supernaturally is so common in Argentina that in Carlos Annacondia's evangelistic rallies those who have had only one or two teeth filled are not allowed to give public testimony. That is considered a "usual" miracle. Three or more teeth being filled is regarded as "unusual" enough to allow the recipient to take time on the platform and share the blessing with the audience.

I realize some readers may not only be skeptical that unusual miracles are occurring now, as they did in Paul's time, but also at this point they may be doubting Peter Wagner's credibility. One of my critics says in a book on the subject that he finds my field reports "preposterous." My response is that I have seen much of what I am reporting firsthand, and for the rest I have spoken extensively with many Argentine friends who are distinguished leaders, well educated, deeply spiritual, highly intelligent—in a word, credible witnesses. They are reporting exactly what they have seen.

Speaking of filling teeth, recent visits to Brazil, where divine dental work has also become common, have allowed me to see with my own eyes something even more unusual. Whereas in Argentina the teeth are most frequently filled with a white sub-stance that dentists cannot identify, in Brazil the great majority are filled or crowned with gold! On my last visit to Brazil, I acquired a book wholly devoted to this phenomenon: *Dentes de Ouro: Os Sinais de Deus* (Gold Teeth: Signs of God) by Pastor Andres Aguiar. Many such stories are documented in the book.

Deliverance Through Handkerchiefs

Back to Ephesus. One of the **unusual miracles was that even handkerchiefs or aprons were brought from his [Paul's] body to the sick,...and the evil spirits went out of them (vv. 11,12).**

Lest we also relegate such things as the use of handkerchiefs to a dim and perhaps irrelevant past, I have but to cite my friend William Kumuyi, pastor of the Deeper Life Bible Church in Lagos, Nigeria. Some 75,000 adults attend his local church on Sundays (and 40,000 children in a building across the street), and he has also planted more than 4,500 other churches around Nigeria. Considering these credentials, he was invited to be the speaker for our annual Fuller Seminary Church Growth Lectures in 1993.

Part of the usual weekly program in all of the 4,500 Deeper Life Bible Churches is a Thursday-night miracle meeting. On one of those nights, the pastor of an outlying church felt led to invite all those who had sick people at home to hold up their handkerchiefs, and he prayed a blessing of God's healing power upon them. They were to return home, place the handkerchief on the sick person and pray for healing in Jesus' name. He was unaware that the chief of a nearby Muslim village was visiting his church that night—the first time he had ever attended a Christian service. Although the Muslim did not have sick people in his home, he also held up his handkerchief and received the blessing.

Soon after the chief had returned to his village, a nine-year-old girl died and he went to her home to attend the wake just before the burial. While there, he suddenly remembered the handkerchief, retrieved it, placed it on the corpse and prayed that she would be healed in Jesus' name. Then God did an obviously "unusual" miracle and raised the girl from the dead! The chief called an immediate ad hoc meeting with the village elders who had witnessed what had happened, then turned around and declared to his people: "For many years we have been serving Mohammed; but from this moment on our village will be a village of Jesus!" Needless to say, a Deeper Life Bible Church is now thriving in the village.

The experience in Nigeria is reminiscent of what Paul was seeing in Ephesus. Ministry was happening not only in word, but also in deed. I like what Susan Garrett says about Ephesus: These unusual miracles were "consistent with the message [Paul] preaches, indeed as part and parcel of that message."[14]

How Not to Do Ground-Level Warfare

....

13. Then some of the itinerant Jewish exorcists took it upon themselves to call the name of the Lord Jesus over

> those who had evil spirits, saying, "We exorcise
> you by the Jesus whom Paul preaches."
> 14. Also there were seven sons of Sceva,
> a Jewish chief priest, who did so.
> 15. And the evil spirit answered and said,
> "Jesus I know, and Paul I know; but who are you?"
> 16. Then the man in whom the evil spirit was leaped on
> them, overpowered them, and prevailed against them, so
> that they fled out of that house naked and wounded.

There is a right way and a wrong way to confront demons. Paul was doing it right, but the seven sons of Sceva did it wrong. The central issue here is the name of the Lord Jesus.

As all who minister deliverance regularly know, the use of the name of Jesus is crucial. Jesus said, "If you ask anything in My name, I will do it" (John 14:14). He also said that among the signs that follow believers: "In My name they will cast out demons" (Mark 16:17). The only authority we have to cast out demons does not reside inside us naturally; it is delegated to us by Jesus. This is similar to the authority a United States ambassador has in a foreign country. Ambassadors do not go to other countries in their own names; they go in the name of the president of the United States. And only those whom the president designates can use his name effectively. If I went to the Japanese Foreign Ministry, for example, and announced that I come in the name of the president of the United States, they would laugh at me.

This is exactly what happened to the seven sons of Sceva. The name of Jesus is no magic formula on the order of the "Ephesian writings," which presumably could be purchased in the neighborhood occult shop. Jesus had not authorized the seven sons of Sceva to use His name and, therefore, the power was absent.

Jesus said that in the last days some will say, "Have we not...cast out demons in Your name?" And He will reply, "I never knew you" (Matt. 7:22,23). That is what He would have said to the sons of Sceva.

Because they used the Lord's name in vain, the seven sons opened themselves to a ferocious spiritual backlash they would not soon forget. They were stripped, beat up and chased out of the house naked!

Occult-Level Spiritual Warfare

....

19:19. Also, many of those who had practiced magic brought their books together and burned them in the sight of all. And they counted up the value of them, and it totaled fifty thousand pieces of silver.

....

Was there a significant relationship between the incident with the seven sons of Sceva and the conversion of the magicians? Susan Garrett thinks so, and says that "the obvious answer is that in Luke's understanding, the Ephesians perceived the defeat of the seven sons to be a defeat of magic in general."[15] Clinton Arnold adds: "The overriding characteristic of the practice of magic throughout the Hellenistic world was the cognizance of a spirit world exercising influence over virtually every aspect of life...there can be no question that spirit beings were perceived as the functionaries behind the magic."[16] This means that, among other things, casting out demons from individuals on the ground level directly influenced the activity of the magicians on the occult level.

Burning Books

The major visible result of the spiritual warfare on the occult-level was a huge public book burning. How many magicians had come to Christ and were annulling their contracts with the spirit world we do not know. But it must have been quite a few, so many that the meager information Luke gives us could reasonably be extrapolated into a possible people movement. Why do I say this?

Let's look at the value of the books and undoubtedly much other occult paraphernalia along with them. All together, they were worth **fifty thousand pieces of silver**. Ernst Haenchen says that "a value equivalent to 50,000 days' wages goes up in flames."[17] If each piece of silver represents a day's wage, in today's terms at $10 an hour for eight-hour days, or $80 a day, it would total $4 million. Quite a book burning!

What should be our attitude toward book burning today? It seems important in Luke's account because he stops to give reports of conversions right before:

> **18. And many who had believed came confessing and telling their deeds.**

And right afterward:

> **20. So the word of the Lord grew mightily and prevailed.**

A similar modern-day book-burning initiative in which the Word of the Lord grew mightily was the three-year evangelistic strategy implemented in Resistencia, Argentina, by Ed Silvoso's Harvest Evangelism organization in the early 1990s. The evangelical community in Resistencia in those three years, and two more years following, grew some 500 percent—remarkable church growth in any nation! As part of the series of evangelistic rallies held at the end of the three-year period, a book-burning ceremony was held every evening, the first such activity I have been able to find on record in any part of Latin America.

Silvoso describes the event as follows: "In anticipation of an Ephesus-type response, a 100-gallon drum was set up to the left of the platform for the new converts to dispose of satanic paraphernalia. As people came forward, they dumped all kinds of occult-related items into it. Before praying for the people, gasoline was poured on the contents of the drum, a match was struck and every evil thing inside went up in flames. Many times, spontaneous deliverances occurred when a specific fetish was burned and the spell was broken."[18]

I wonder what new doors to evangelism might be opened in sophisticated, tolerant, politically correct America if Christians started expressing their faith by encouraging those who possessed artifacts of magic or unclean books to burn them publicly? Only one pastor I am aware of at the moment is doing this regularly. Pastor Donovan Larkins of Spirit of Life Christian Center in Dayton, Ohio, takes his congregation out every Halloween night for public book burnings, much to the consternation of the local authorities, as well as some of the other church leaders in his city. In his book, *Up In Smoke*, Larkins says, "This type of public display is a witness of total rejection of Satan's kingdom and total allegiance to Jesus Christ and the kingdom of God!"[19]

Susan Garrett says something similar: "Luke's purpose...[was] to emphasize the sweeping victory of the Lord over the powers of darkness even in Ephesus, noted center of the magical arts."[20]

Strategic-Level Spiritual Warfare

The principal focal point of strategic-level spiritual warfare in Ephesus was Diana of the Ephesians, which is her Latin name,

the Greek equivalent being Artemis. I am going to use the name
"Diana," which is used in *The New King James Version*. It is
important to know some details about this extraordinary princi-
pality of darkness. To begin with, the distraught silversmiths are
saying:

27. So not only is this trade of ours in danger of
falling into disrepute, but also the temple of the great
goddess Diana may be despised and her magnificence
destroyed, whom all Asia and the world worship.
28. Now when they heard this, they were full of wrath
and cried out, saying, "Great is Diana of the Ephesians!"

The language here is exquisite: **great goddess...her magnificence...all Asia and the world worship** [her]. She is said to be
worthy of people crying, **"Great is Diana of the Ephesians!"**
Clinton Arnold says Diana "was worshipped more widely by individuals than any other deity known to Pausanius."[21]

Diana as a Territorial Spirit

If we are indeed dealing with strategic-level spiritual warfare in
this passage, it is necessary to explain why Diana may be regarded, not just as another demon, but as a territorial spirit. By territorial spirit, I mean a high-ranking member of the hierarchy of
evil spirits delegated by Satan to control a nation, region, tribe,
city, people group, neighborhood or any other significant social
network of human beings.

Artemis had wide influence throughout the Roman Empire.
F. F. Bruce makes reference to K. Wernicke who "enumerates
thirty-three places, all over the known world, where Ephesian
Artemis was venerated."[22] Even so, her chief location, which

might have been called a seat of Satan, was Ephesus. Paul Trebilco, a New Zealand biblical scholar, says, "While Ephesus was the home of many cults, the most significant and powerful deity was Artemis of Ephesus."[23]

Why might we conceive of Diana as a territorial spirit over Ephesus? For one thing, "Artemis" is the name given to her by the Greeks, but it is not a Greek name. She was actually ruling Ephesus before the Greeks arrived.[24] For another, Diana's influence on all aspects of life in Ephesus was notable. Trebilco says, "It was the cult of the Ephesian Artemis which, more than anything else, made Ephesus a centre of religious life during our period. But the influence of the cult of Artemis extended beyond the religious sphere to the civic, economic, and cultural life of the city."[25] This fits our working definition of a territorial spirit. Apropos to strategic-level spiritual warfare, which seeks to engage such spirits and challenge their authority, Trebilco says, "Any factor which sidelined Artemis would affect not only the religious, but also virtually all facets of life of the city."[26] In other words, part of effectively reaching Ephesus for God would necessarily include breaking the power of this all-controlling demon.

Some of the blasphemous names given to Diana were "greatest," "holiest," "most manifest," "Lady," "Savior" and "Queen of the Cosmos."[27] It is not farfetched to identify her—as we suggested in the case of Athena, the territorial spirit over Athens—with the infamous "queen of heaven" found in Jeremiah 7:16-18.

The Demonic Art and Architecture

As Paul stressed in his speech in the Athens Areopagus, two of the chief ways humans frequently honor demonic spirits is through art and architecture. This was true in Ephesus. Diana's image, designed to glorify the creature rather than the Creator, was ubiquitous throughout the city. Unexpectedly, it was not pretty, but grotesque. It was more like an ugly Asian idol rather than a beautiful work of Greek art because, as I have mentioned, she had been worshiped in Ephesus even before the Greeks arrived. Clinton Arnold points out a significant characteristic: She was "the only divinity to depict visibly her divine superiority with the signs of the zodiac."[28]

The temple of Diana was anything but ugly. It was one of the most beautiful pieces of architecture in history, one of the seven wonders of the ancient world. It contained 93,500 square feet, four times the size of the Parthenon in Athens. It was supported by 127 columns, each one was 60 feet high and donated by a different king. Conybeare and Howson say, "The sun, it was said, saw nothing in its course more magnificent than Diana's temple....It is probable that there was no religious building in the world in which was concentrated a greater amount of admiration, enthusiasm, and superstition."[29] In other words, the temple was a center of awesome spiritual power emanating from the invisible world of darkness.

Two major annual festivals honored Diana and reaffirmed to her and to the rest of the spirit world that the residents of Ephesus desired to continue to do her bidding for another year. One festival, the Artemisia, lasted a whole month. The other festival celebrated her birthday because supposedly she had been born near Ephesus. It was said that "this was one of the largest and most magnificent religious celebrations in Ephesus' liturgical calendar."[30]

The Riot

19:23. And about that time there arose a
great commotion about the Way.

Considering that spiritual warfare was occurring at all levels, and victory after victory was being achieved by the forces of the kingdom of God, things could not long remain quiet in Ephesus. As John Stott says, "It was inevitable that sooner or later the kingly authority of Jesus would challenge Diana's evil sway."[31] The magnitude of the riot is one more indication of Diana's territorial power. She was no ordinary demon.

---

24. For a certain man named Demetrius,
a silversmith, who made silver shrines of Diana,
brought no small profit to the craftsmen.
25. He called them together with the workers of
similar occupation, and said, "Men, you know that
we have our prosperity by this trade.
26. Moreover you see and hear that not only at Ephesus,
but throughout almost all Asia, this Paul has persuaded
and turned away many people, saying that they are
not gods which are made with hands.
27. So not only is this trade of ours in danger of falling
into disrepute, but also the temple of the great goddess
Diana may be despised and her magnificence destroyed,
whom all Asia and the world worship."

The problem was ostensibly an economic and a cultural one. But deeper than that, it was a spiritual problem. The territorial spirit who had been unmolested for centuries was losing her power! Why was she losing power? So many of the magicians whom she had controlled had been losing their battles in occult-level spiritual warfare against the Christians that control of the city was slipping out of her hands. Clinton Arnold says, "Although it has been claimed that the Ephesian Artemis was not by nature a goddess of magic, she does seem to have had a direct link with the magical practices of the time."[32] Her evil power could no longer control the local web of magic.

> 29. So the whole city was filled with confusion, and
> rushed into the theater with one accord,...
> 34. ...all with one voice cried out for about two
> hours, "Great is Diana of the Ephesians!"
> 35. And when the city clerk had quieted the crowd,
> he said: "Men of Ephesus,...
> 37. For you have brought these men here who are neither
> robbers of temples nor blasphemers of your goddess.
> 38. Therefore if Demetrius and his fellow craftsmen
> have a case against anyone, the courts are open and
> there are proconsuls...."
> 41. And when he said these things, he dismissed
> the assembly.

The accusations against Paul were without substance. The city clerk of Ephesus justly cut through the emotional fog being raised by the silversmiths and dismissed the case.

Confronting Diana: Paul Versus John

During his ministry in Ephesus, Paul and his coworkers had succeeded in binding Diana, the territorial spirit, so that the gospel could spread. But they did this without directly confronting her (**these men are not blasphemers of your goddess**) nor doing warfare in her temple (**neither robbers of temples**). Paul was not averse to doing such a thing because he previously confronted the Python spirit in Philippi directly (see 16:18), but this was neither the time nor the place for a confrontation.

After the book of Acts closes and history picks up, we come to Scene II of this drama in Ephesus. Some years later, after Paul had left, the apostle John takes up residence in Ephesus. According to Ramsay MacMullen, a historian, John, unlike Paul, eventually did enter directly into the famous temple of Diana to do strategic-level spiritual warfare. In the temple, he prayed this prayer: "O God...at whose name every idol takes flight and every demon and every unclean power: now let the demon that is here [i.e., Diana] take flight in thy name!"[33]

And what happened? History again tells us that when John took authority over Diana, her altar immediately split into pieces and half the temple crumbled to the ground! This is such an extraordinary report that some might question its historical reliability. Anticipating this, Ramsay MacMullen hastens to say, "I don't think the explanatory force of this scene should be discounted on the grounds that it cannot have really happened, that it is fiction, that no one was meant to believe it."[34]

Why did John take on Diana directly, but Paul did not? I think the answer is simple. God's timing is absolutely crucial for doing responsible strategic-level spiritual warfare, as I have often stressed. When Paul was in Ephesus, God did not tell him to do it because, for reasons we may never know, it was not yet time. Contrariwise, God did tell John to do it because it was then the proper time. It is likely that if Paul had tried what John did, he would have failed the same way the seven sons of Sceva did!

The Demise of Diana

The one-two punches by Paul and John, as well as the prayers and aggressive spiritual warfare that must have been occurring among the believers in Ephesus before and after, had sealed the doom of the cult of Diana. An inscription written by a believer in Ephesus reads, in part, "Destroying the delusive image of the demon Artemis, Demeas has erected this symbol of Truth, the God that drives away idols, and the Cross of priests, deathless and victorious sign of Christ."[35]

Although records indicate that the worship of Diana still enthralled many people for at least 50 years after John had faced her one-on-one, she didn't last much longer than that. Clinton Arnold finds that "the influx and expansion of Christianity eventually wrought the demise of the cult of the Ephesian Artemis."[36]

The First Blazes in Ephesus and Asia Minor

17. This became known both to all Jews and Greeks dwelling in Ephesus; and fear fell on them all, and the name of the Lord Jesus was magnified.
18. And many who had believed came confessing and telling of their deeds.
20. So the word of the Lord grew mightily and prevailed.

We will want to remember once again that as the gospel spread across the city of Ephesus and its quarter-million inhabitants, the believers did not gather weekly in one huge megachurch. Instead, many house churches would have been meeting in many parts of the city, and those churches would have been multiplying under their own momentum. These would not have been confined only to Ephesus city, but they presumably would also be multiplying in the immediate suburbs such as Metropolis, Hypaipa, Diashieron, Neikaia, Koloe and Palaiapolis, according to Clinton Arnold.[37]

Paul's enemies also recognized that these churches were rapidly spreading into other cities in Asia. Demetrius the silversmith laments that **throughout almost all Asia, this Paul has persuaded and turned away many people** (v. 26).

From what we can surmise, Paul himself stayed in Ephesus city for the three years, training the church planters who would then move out into the other parts of Asia. Some evidence for this comes from the Epistle Paul later wrote to one of those cities—Colossae. In Colossians, Paul mentions that the Christians there had never seen him in person, and neither had the believers in another one of Asia's cities—Laodicia (see Col. 2:1).

Who were the church planters who graduated from what we have been playfully calling The Siesta Theological Seminary? Many, if not most, we will never know, but we do have the names of some of the alumni: Epaphras (see Col. 1:7), Tychicus (see Acts 20:4; Eph. 6:21; Col. 4:7), Trophimus (see Acts 20:4), Philemon (see Philem. 1:1) and Archippus (see Philem. 1:2).

What churches did they plant? Again, our list is not complete, but we can name several: Colossae, Laodicia, Hierapolis, and the ones other than Ephesus listed in Revelation 2—3: Smyrna, Pergamos, Thyatira, Sardis and Philadelphia. F. F. Bruce notes, "The province [of Asia] was intensely evangelized and remained one of the leading centers of Christianity for many centuries."[38]

Occupying Diana's Territory

I titled this chapter "Invading Diana's Territory" because it is the clearest biblical example I have found of a well-known territorial spirit being engaged by the forces of the kingdom of God and losing control of the territory. In this case, Paul had literally fulfilled the mandate he had received from Jesus on the Damascus road to turn Gentiles **from darkness to light, and from the power of Satan to God** (Acts 26:18).

Although it is true that the seat of Diana's power was Ephesus city, her territorial jurisdiction apparently extended throughout the province of Asia. Clinton Arnold affirms that "[Diana] was worshipped in...the cities of Colossae, Laodicia, and Hierapolis" and that "the grandeur and fame of the temple of Diana was only exceeded by the influence of the cult itself, not only in Ephesus, but throughout all of Asia."[39]

Not everyone, perhaps including Clinton Arnold himself, would necessarily draw from this the conclusion that Diana was, indeed, a territorial spirit. Nevertheless, it looks very much that way to me, especially considering the suggestion that the temple of Diana, one of the seven wonders of the ancient world, was *surpassed* by the spiritual power of her cult throughout the province. Imagine the control this demonic ruler had freely exercised over the souls of millions of human beings throughout the centuries! This is exactly what is implied by the modern term "territorial spirit."

In this last recorded episode of Paul's church-planting missionary career, we see his most outstanding victory. With the power and authority of Jesus Christ, he had invaded a territory that Satan had ruled from time immemorial. Paul was not wrestling against flesh and blood, but, as he later said, "against principalities, against powers, against the rulers of the darkness of this age, against spiritual hosts of wickedness in the heavenly places" (Eph. 6:12). As a result, Diana's territory was not only invaded, it was also conquered!

As I said in the beginning of this chapter, Acts 19 is one of my favorite chapters in the Bible. If Acts truly is "A Training Manual for Every Christian," as I contend, no chapter in Acts could be more helpful for learning principles of evangelism and more encouraging regarding potential results for those willing to move into enemy territory by the power of the Holy Spirit!

Reflection Questions

1. Ephesus was a center of magic where fetishes were manufactured. What have you seen that could be identified as a fetish?
   Do these really have some kind of supernatural power?
2. Why was training church planters more important to Paul in
   Ephesus than going through the surrounding cities of Asia
   and conducting evangelistic crusades? How would you apply
   this to missions today?
3. How much weight should we put on the findings of historians
   such as Ramsay MacMullen? They do not carry the authority
   of Scripture, but what authority do you think they carry?
4. Do you think that reports of teeth being filled supernaturally
   in Argentina and Brazil are "preposterous," as one person
   says? Why or why not?
5. What would you think of Christian leaders in your city orga-
   nizing and endorsing public burnings of evil items as they did
   in Ephesus? What would some of the sensible ground rules of
   such an initiative be?

Notes
   1. E. M. Blaiklock, *Acts: The Birth of the Church* (Grand Rapids:
      Fleming H. Revell Company, 1980), p. 185.
   2. Clinton E. Arnold, *Ephesians: Power and Magic* (Grand Rapids:
      Baker Book House, 1992), p. 6.
   3. Quoted in Paul Trebilco, "Asia," *The Book of Acts in Its Graeco-
      Roman Setting*, ed. David W. J. Gill and Conrad Gempf (Grand
      Rapids: William B. Eerdmans Publishing Company, 1994), pp.
      305-306.
   4. Bruce M. Metzger, "St. Paul and the Magicians," *Princeton*

Seminary Bulletin 38 (June 1944): 27.

5. F. F. Bruce, *Paul: Apostle of the Heart Set Free* (Grand Rapids: William B. Eerdmans Publishing Company, 1977), p. 291.

6. William Mitchell Ramsay, *St. Paul the Traveller and the Roman Citizen* (London, England: Hodder & Stoughton, 1925), p. 271.

7. Arnold, *Ephesians*, p. 1.

8. Bruce, *Paul*, p. 295.

9. Michael Green, *Evangelism in the Early Church* (Grand Rapids: William B. Eerdmans Publishing Company, 1970), pp. 188-189.

10. Ramsay MacMullen, *Christianizing the Roman Empire* (New Haven, Conn.: Yale University Press, 1984), p. 28.

11. Ibid., p. 112.

12. Ibid., p. 113.

13. Susan R. Garrett says, "I will argue...that Luke uses the story of the seven sons of Sceva...to advance the theme of the ongoing Christian triumph over Satan, and, consequently, over magic." *The Demise of the Devil* (Minneapolis: Fortress Press, 1989), p. 90.

14. Ibid., p. 91.

15. Ibid., p. 95.

16. Arnold, *Ephesians*, p. 18.

17. Ernst Haenchen, *The Acts of the Apostles: A Commentary* (Philadelphia, Pa.: The Westminster Press, 1971), p. 567.

18. Ed Silvoso, *That None Should Perish* (Ventura, Calif.: Regal Books, 1994), p. 50.

19. Donovan A. Larkins, *Up In Smoke: Why I Conduct Public Book Burnings* (Victory Press Publications, P.O. Box 7064, Dayton, OH 45407, 1994), p. 44.

20. Garrett, *The Demise of the Devil*, p. 97.

21. Arnold, *Ephesians*, p. 20.

22. F. F. Bruce, *The Book of Acts* (Grand Rapids: William B. Eerdmans Publishing Company, 1988; revised edition, 1954), p. 375.

23. Trebilco, "Asia," *The Book of Acts in Its Graeco-Roman Setting*, p. 316.

24. See Bruce, *The Book of Acts*, p. 373.

25. Trebilco, "Asia," *The Book of Acts in Its Graeco-Roman Setting*, p. 316.

26. Ibid., p. 329.

27. Ibid., pp. 317-318.
28. Arnold, *Ephesians*, p. 21.
29. W. J. Conybeare and J. S. Howson, *The Life and Epistles of St. Paul* (London, England: Longmans, Green and Co., 1875), p. 423.
30. Trebilco, "Asia," *The Book of Acts in Its Graeco-Roman Setting*, p. 321.
31. John Stott, *The Spirit, The Church and the World: The Message of Acts* (Downers Grove, Ill.: InterVarsity Press, 1990), p. 308.
32. Arnold, *Ephesians*, p. 22
33. MacMullen, *Christianizing the Roman Empire*, p. 26.
34. Ibid.
35. Ibid., p. 18.
36. Arnold, *Ephesians*, p. 28.
37. Ibid., p. 6.
38. Bruce, *The Book of Acts*, p. 366.
39. Arnold, *Ephesians*, p. 20.

A Long Trip Toward the Jerusalem Jail

Beginning with Acts 20, Luke shifts gears decisively in his historical account of the spread of the gospel through the ancient world by the ministry of the apostles. In the remaining nine chapters of his book, Luke gives us very little more information about missiology, church planting or power ministries. Not that these are absent, for we have some important things yet to learn about these crucial issues. But we will find that Luke's major emphasis is elsewhere, concentrating more on Paul's experiences of being jailed and defending himself in several courtroom-type scenes. In this respect, Luke concludes Acts much as he also does his Gospel.

Because of this, readers may have noticed that a relatively small number of pages remain in this three-volume work. According to my calculations, I am devoting only 8 percent of my full commentary on Acts to these nine chapters, which in turn comprise 32 percent of Luke's original work. As points of comparison, F. F. Bruce uses 26 percent of his commentary for these final chapters and John Stott only 22 percent. But as a reminder, my chief purpose for writing this 1,399th commentary on Acts is to highlight precisely the areas of missiology and power ministries that are not particularly stressed in the other 1,398. From now on, Luke's focus on missiology and power ministries are few and far between, so I will be moving rapidly over some of Luke's text.

Paul Never Lost His Vision

From this point on, Paul had to expend much energy to defend himself and the faith he represented. He spent a great deal of time in custody, but he never lost the vision Jesus had given him on the Damascus road. As one of his final missionary tasks, he had established an important center for Christianity in the city of Ephesus. Here are some significant features of Ephesus:

1. Paul wrote 1 Corinthians from Ephesus.
2. Timothy succeeded Paul in Ephesus. Paul wrote 1 and 2 Timothy to him while Timothy was in Ephesus (see 1 Tim. 1:3).
3. The apostle John later took up residence in Ephesus and wrote 1, 2 and 3 John from there, as well as the Gospel of John. I could well imagine that the seminary Paul had started in Tyrannus's school building had included both Timothy and John on the faculty, as well as many others as the years passed.
4. Paul planned his future there:

19:21. When these things were accomplished, Paul purposed in the Spirit, when he had passed through

> Macedonia and Achaia, to go to Jerusalem, saying, "After
> I have been there, I must also see Rome."

Visiting the established churches in Achaia (which would include its capital, Corinth) and in Macedonia (which would include Philippi, Thessalonica and Berea) was important for Paul. But, avoiding the "syndrome of church development," which we have mentioned from time to time, his true vision was for Rome, which he had never visited. Not only that, but we later also learn that Rome, in Paul's mind, was considered just a stopping-off place because Christian churches had already been planted and were multiplying in Rome. He really wanted to pioneer the work in Spain.

In his letter to the Christians in Rome, Paul says, "For this reason I also have been much hindered from coming to you. But now no longer having a place in these parts, and having a great desire these many years to come to you, whenever I journey to Spain, I shall come to you" (Rom. 15:22-24). Paul also tells the Romans that he hopes they will provide financial support for his projected missionary work in Spain: "I hope to...be helped on my way there by you" (v. 24).

No one knows for sure whether Paul ever made it to Spain. But whether he did or not, he never lost his vision for frontier missions. As F. F. Bruce says, "[Paul] looked around for fresh worlds to conquer."[1]

Encouraging Friends
Acts 20

> 20:1. After the uproar [in Ephesus] had ceased,
> Paul called the disciples to himself, embraced them,

and departed to go to Macedonia.
2. Now when he had gone over that region and encour·
aged them with many words, he came to Greece
3. and stayed three months....

From this account, it looks as though Paul went directly from Ephesus to Philippi (**Macedonia**). But, no—Luke chooses not to mention that Paul first went back to Troas where he originally had received the Macedonian vision to go to Philippi and other parts of Europe for the first time (see 16:8,9). We learn this not from Acts, but from Paul himself when he later writes 2 Corinthians: "Furthermore, when I came to Troas to preach Christ's gospel, and a door was opened to me by the Lord, I had no rest in my spirit, because I did not find Titus my brother; but taking my leave of them, I departed for Macedonia" (2:12,13).

First, then, he went to Troas to preach and there he found good receptivity—an open door to the gospel. But Paul also expressed a bit of frustration when he didn't meet Titus there as expected. As we read Acts, it seems strange that Luke does not mention Titus at all. He is well known to us because a letter later written to him by Paul has become one of the books of our New Testament. This is a puzzle to many. William Ramsay says, "The complete omission of Titus' name must be intentional." But no one seems to know why. "It is equally hard to explain on every theory," adds Ramsay.[2]

Paul then set out for Macedonia and the city of Philippi where he had previously sent Timothy and Erastus from Ephesus (see Acts 19:22). It seems that he stayed there quite a while, possibly a year and a half, according to F. F. Bruce.[3] This is an unusually long period of time to spend in an already existing church, given what we have said about the need to avoid the "syndrome of church development." Why would Paul have done this?

It could be that Paul moved in with Luke and Lydia, became very comfortable, had his material needs cared for without making tents, and enjoyed some leisure time while also meeting with and instructing the believers. He also wrote 2 Corinthians while he was in Philippi.

But this does not sound like what we would usually expect of this restless frontier missionary we have been following. Another possible explanation why Paul stayed in Philippi so long seems more feasible to me. Toward the end of his letter to the Romans Paul writes, "For I will not dare to speak of any of those things which Christ has not accomplished through me, in word and deed, to make Gentiles obedient in mighty signs and wonders, by the power of the Spirit of God, so that from Jerusalem and round about to Illyricum I have fully preached the gospel of Christ" (15:18,19). This sounds more like what we have come to expect of Paul, and the interesting thing is that he specifies "Illyricum."

Illyricum is the province to the north of Macedonia, occupying much of the lands of the former Yugoslavia. Luke doesn't mention it in Acts, and nowhere else do we find a reference about when Paul might have preached in Illyricum. This is one logical place to surmise that Paul could have used Philippi as a base from which he moved out to plant churches throughout the regions north of Philippi. This is the time when Paul probably reached his northernmost evangelistic targets.

Luke does not tell of this either, but it turns out that Titus had actually been in Corinth, and that he and Paul were reunited here in Philippi (see 2 Cor. 7:5-7) instead of in Troas as Paul had first expected. Because, for whatever reason, Luke chooses not to mention Titus, we could conjecture that Titus went to Illyricum with Paul and that could be the reason none of this is mentioned in Acts.

Fund-Raising in Corinth

When Paul left Philippi, it is likely that Timothy and Erastus accompanied him to Corinth. Whether he had also visited churches in Thessalonica and Berea while in Macedonia we do not know, but the words **when he had gone over that region** (Acts 20:2) sound as if he might have. One purpose could have been to raise funds, as we shall soon see. In any case, Paul spent the winter of A.D. 56-57 in Corinth, undoubtedly encouraging the believers as he had done in Macedonia.

Paul had the gift of apostle, and, thereby, he had a great deal of authority over the churches in his jurisdiction. Simon Kistemaker observes, "Paul was the spiritual father of the believers in the Gentile world, and he addressed them as his spiritual children."[4] The church in Corinth, from the evidence we have in 1 Corinthians, had become one of the most messed-up churches with which Paul had to deal. In that letter, written from Ephesus, Paul had clearly laid out two options for them: "What do you want? Shall I come to you with a rod, or in love and a spirit of gentleness?" (4:21).

The answer was that the Corinthians themselves decided to clean up their act before Paul got there, and Titus had brought this good news to Paul while he was still in Philippi. The good news prompted Paul to write 2 Corinthians, in which he said, "God,...comforted us by the coming of Titus, and not only by his coming, but also by the consolation with which he was comforted in you, when he told us of your earnest desire, your mourning, your zeal for me, so that I rejoiced even more" (7:6,7).

We also learn from 2 Corinthians that Paul was on his way to Corinth to raise funds. The believers in Jerusalem were struggling. The scenario we read about in Acts 2, where the believers "sold their possessions and goods, and divided them among all, as anyone had need" (v. 45), had changed radically when the wealthier Hellenistic Jewish believers were driven out of Jerusalem as a backlash from Stephen's ministry (see 8:1), leaving only the poorer Hebrew Jewish believers. Paul refers to them when he says, "Now concerning the ministering to the saints" (2 Cor. 9:1).

Some Principles of Fund-Raising

Paul's visit to Corinth prompted some of the most detailed principles of fund-raising we have in the Scriptures. If we follow Paul's lead, we will keep three things in mind:

• *Let Christians know what others are doing.* It seems Paul did not believe donation records should be kept secret. He told the Corinthians that the churches in Macedonia, although they were poor, gave generously to the fund. "For I bear witness that according to their ability, yes, and beyond their ability, they were freely willing" (2 Cor. 8:3). This is not designed to put individuals or churches in competition with one another. The intention is to build each other's faith.

• *Giving is like sowing seed.* The more you sow, the more you reap. "He who sows sparingly will also reap sparingly, and he who sows bountifully will also reap bountifully" (9:6). Is this a teaching about prosperity? If prosperity means greediness and the desire to have money to support an opulent lifestyle, it certainly does not. But if prosperity means having sufficient resources for living, plus much more to give to others, it apparently means just that. I like the way the *Good News Bible* translates 2 Corinthians 9:8, "And God is able to give you more than you need, so that you will always have all you need for yourselves and more than enough for every good cause."

• *Giving causes joy.* "God loves a cheerful giver" (v. 7). I am well acquainted with many Christians who are generous givers, contributing much more than the expected tithe, or 10 percent of income, to "every good cause." I have not yet found one of them who is not a cheerful giver nor have I found one for whom God has not provided all the necessities of life. Not all, but some, are subsequently able to live more comfortable lives than many of the more stingy believers around them. In most cases, increased giving causes increased cheerfulness, not the other way around.

Fleeing the Jews Again

20:3. ...And when the Jews plotted against him as he was about to sail to Syria, he decided to return through Macedonia.

The Jews in Corinth, who were previously unsuccessful in having Paul accused of breaking the Roman law by Gallio, now set out on a more direct approach to attack Paul. They decided to take the law into their own hands. Paul, therefore, changed his plans and did not head directly for Jerusalem. William Ramsay says, "With a shipload of hostile Jews, it would be easy to find opportunity to murder Paul."[5]

Paul might have also had a word directly from God in making this decision. Although we do not have it in our version, another ancient text of the New Testament, which scholars do not ignore, says, "The Spirit told him to return through Macedonia."

Back in Philippi (Macedonia), a regional leadership meeting is taking place. Seven people from a variety of churches in the area have gathered to prepare to take their relief funds to Jerusalem. The seven then continued on to Troas while Paul and Luke stayed for a time in Philippi. We know Luke was there because the passage from Acts shifts to the first person "we" at this point:

> **5. These men, going ahead, waited for us at Troas.**

A Week at Troas

> **7. Now on the first day of the week, when the disciples [in Troas] came together to break bread, Paul, ready to depart the next day, spoke to them and continued his message until midnight.**

Many of the commentators who write about this passage draw the conclusion from the phrase **"the first day of the week, when the disciples came together to break bread"** that by this time in A.D. 57, Sunday worship had become normal for Christians. The traditional worship day for the Jews, of course, was Saturday—the Sabbath or the last day of the week. Although Seventh-day Adventists and others continue to keep the Sabbath, most Christians conduct their primary worship services on Sunday. The roots of this, interestingly enough, go back largely to custom and consensus rather than to explicit biblical mandate. In the particular case of Troas, it could be argued just as strongly that the reason the Christians met the *first* day of the week was that Paul's ship was scheduled to sail the *second* day of the week. It could well have been a farewell party, highlighted perhaps by the Lord's Supper.

Some, I know, may be uncomfortable with this observation. But the two other biblical passages frequently cited to justify Sunday worship, 1 Corinthians 16:2 and John 20:19, furnish, at best, circumstantial evidence subject to shades of interpretation. We need to recognize that many other deeply established

Christian beliefs and practices do not have explicit biblical mandates either. Examples include referring to God as "Trinity," freeing slaves, casting demons out of Christians, erecting church buildings, strategic-level spiritual warfare and even praying for lost people to be saved. None of these is contrary to Scripture, and we practice them in most of our churches because we have long ago concluded that the circumstantial evidence we do have for these things directs us to do them in conformity with the general sense of Scripture and the will of God.

In any case, it is known that Christians early on decided they should worship on Sunday to honor the Lord's resurrection on the first day of the week. By the end of the first century, Sunday was being called the "Lord's Day," according to *The Didache*, an ancient record of the apostles' teachings (*Didache 14:1*). Whether this was the reason for this meeting in Troas, however, is questionable.

Raising the Dead

8. There were many lamps in the upper room
where they were gathered together.

9. And in a window sat a certain young man named
Eutychus, who was sinking into a deep sleep. He was
overcome by sleep; and as Paul continued speaking, he
fell down from the third story and was taken up dead.

10. But Paul went down, fell on him, and embracing him
said, "Do not trouble yourselves, for his life is in him."

11. Now when he had come up, had broken bread
and eaten, and talked a long while, even till daybreak,
he departed.

12. And they brought the young man in alive,
and they were not a little comforted.

This is the last of nine examples we have in the Bible of the dead being raised. For the record, here they are:

1. Elijah raises a young boy (see 1 Kings 17:17-24)
2. Elisha raises a young boy (see 2 Kings 4:32-37)
3. Jesus raises a widow's grown son (see Luke 7:11-16)
4. Jesus raises Jairus's daughter (see Luke 8:49-56)
5. Jesus raises Lazarus (see John 11:43,44)
6. Jesus Himself is raised (see Luke 24:6)
7. Peter raises Dorcas (see Acts 9:36-42)
8. Paul is raised through prayers of the believers (see Acts 14:19,20)
9. Paul raises Eutychus (see Acts 20:9-12)

Bible-believing Christians have little reason to deny that dead are still being raised today, as some do. Reports of this occurring have been coming in from many places by credible witnesses, perhaps not daily, but certainly regularly. Jesus commanded His disciples to raise the dead the first time He sent them out on an evangelistic tour (see Matt. 10:8). He then ordered His disciples to teach their converts to do all that He had commanded them (see 28:20), presumably, including raising the dead. Both Peter and Paul did just that, and undoubtedly many others as well in the first century. Interestingly, we have more *biblical* evidence for Christians raising the dead through the power of the Holy Spirit than we have for worshiping on Sunday.

The Pastors' Seminar for Asia

16. For Paul had decided to sail past Ephesus, so that he would not have to spend time in Asia,...
17. From Miletus he sent to Ephesus and called

for the elders of the church.
18. And when they had come to him, he said to them:...

On his way to Jerusalem, Paul wanted to conduct a leadership training seminar for the pastors of the Ephesian churches. Apparently, he did not care to socialize with the believers in general, so he bypassed the city of Ephesus and stopped at Miletus, a two-days' journey by land to the south. This is the only example we have in Acts of Paul's teaching to Christians in general, in this case, specifically to leaders. All other examples of Paul's speeches are directed to evangelize unbelievers, either Jews or Gentiles, or to defend himself in front of government officials and accusers.

Unlike the challenges many of us face today, marketing this seminar was relatively easy. All it took was Paul's announcement that the seminar would be held. The reason for this was Paul's recognized position as an apostle—a position that carried with it an extraordinary amount of spiritual authority, including powers of convocation. Although I have had no similar experience with my pastors' seminars, I have seen it in operation with my friend John Wimber, who, like Paul, has the gift of apostle. If I attract 300 attendees to my seminars, I think I am doing well. If John Wimber calls a leadership seminar for Vineyard pastors and attracts less than 3,000, he thinks he has poor attendance.

Modern readers often do not understand that this is a *pastors'* seminar as opposed to a seminar for lay elders because many English Bible versions, such as *The New King James Version*, which we are using, translate the Greek *presbyteros* as "elders," certainly a legitimate translation. But so many of our churches are structured today with an ordained senior pastor who works with a board of lay elders that "elders" has taken on another meaning. Let me explain.

Three Greek words, all used by Paul in his seminar here in Miletus, refer to the pastors he had called together:

17. ...[Paul] called for the *elders* of the church.
28. "Therefore take heed to yourselves and to all the flock, among which the Holy Spirit has made you *overseers*, to *shepherd* the church of God... (italics mine).

- elders = *presbyteros*. This is the standard word for elders, and the root from which we get the name "Presbyterian Church." It is a church government in which the lay elders rule the local congregation.
- overseers = *episkopos*. We usually translate this as bishops, meaning those who supervise a number of pastors. This is the root word for the "Episcopal Church."
- shepherd = *poimen*. Using the metaphor of the caretaker of sheep, we usually translate this as "pastor."

The point to note here is that all three of these words refer to the same people Paul is teaching, so that at least to a significant extent, we can consider them synonyms for each other. Despite certain individual nuances, these three words denote the top leaders of local churches as opposed to another important kind of church leaders called "deacons." The two are clearly differentiated in 1 Timothy 3, where Paul first lists the qualifications of a bishop (see 3:1-7) and then the qualifications of a deacon (see vv. 8-13).

The House Churches of Ephesus

The leaders who walked for two days from Ephesus to Miletus to attend the seminar were, to sum it up, the pastors of the multiple house churches in Ephesus city, and undoubtedly from the immediate outlying suburbs. Paul refers to the house churches as he speaks to them when, recalling his three-year ministry there, he says he would go **from house to house** (Acts 20:20). It is easy for us in the twentieth century to forget that no such things as church buildings, as we now know them, existed in the Early Church. Bradley Blue says, "The gathering of Christian believers in private homes (or homes renovated for the purpose of Christian gatherings) continued to be the norm until the early decades of the fourth century when Constantine began erecting the first Christian basilicas."[6]

It is important, not just for understanding the nature of Paul's seminar in Miletus, but also for understanding church planting in the book of Acts in general, to look closely at the word "church," which we translate from the Greek *ekklesia*. Few have helped us more on this subject than Robert Banks in his excellent book *Paul's Idea of Community*. Although some may conclude that all the Christians in a large city such as Ephesus would occasionally, if not regularly, meet together, Banks does not agree. He says, "There is no suggestion that Christians ever met as a whole in one place."[7] He goes on to explain the following about *ekklesia* or "church": "The word does not describe all the Christians who live in a particular locality if they do not gather. Nor does it refer to the sum total of Christians in a region or scattered throughout the world at any particular time. And never during this period is the term applied to a building in which Christians meet."[8]

Although it is hard to read the details of our twentieth century back into the first century, it is not farfetched to say that those whom Paul was teaching in his seminar would be the functional equivalent of what we regard today as ordained ministers. Each one would have been in charge of a relatively small congregation meeting in someone's home. I can well imagine that by this time some 200 such congregations might have been meeting in greater Ephesus, considering its population of 250,000 people, in addition to the adjoining suburbs.

Paul's Teaching

How long would this seminar have lasted? One day? Two days? Suppose, just to make a point, it was a one-day seminar and Paul taught for six hours. That means he would have taught for 360 minutes. But Luke summarizes Paul's teaching in Acts 20:18-35, which can be read out loud in 2 minutes and 10 seconds. In other words, we have here less than one-half of 1 percent of Paul's teaching content, even assuming it was a short one-day seminar. So from one perspective, we could say we have ended up with but a brief summary of the high points that seemed important to Luke. Or, from another perspective, we could say we trust that the Holy Spirit, who inspired Luke as he was writing Acts, guided Luke supernaturally to select the exact items that would be the most important for the leaders of the church through the ages. Let's move on this latter assumption.

As I read it, it looks as though the seminar could have been divided into four sessions, all of which are important for Christian leaders in all places at all times:

Session 1: Striving for a servant's heart (Acts 20:17-21).

Just before coming here to Miletus, Paul had written his letters to the Corinthians. In these letters, he makes two statements that every Christian leader who serves as a role model for others should also be able to make:

"I do not even judge myself. For I know nothing against myself, yet I am not justified by this; but He who judges me is the Lord" (1 Cor. 4:3,4). As Paul honestly examined his own life, he could find nothing wrong. This is the basis on which he could later say, "Therefore, I urge you, imitate me" (v. 16). He was not reluctant to use his own life and testimony as a model for Christian leadership. How could the leaders attain this?

> 20:18. ..."You know, from the first day that I came to Asia, in what manner I always lived among you,
> 19. serving the Lord with all humility, with many tears and trials which happened to me by the plotting of the Jews."

Paul regarded himself as a slave, **serving the Lord.** In many other places, he also refers to himself as a slave (see for example Rom. 1:1). Coming from a society in which many of the pastors themselves would undoubtedly either have owned slaves, or have been slaves themselves at the time,* they would have known exactly what he was talking about. They knew that taking the attitude of a slave would invariably produce humility. As they served the Lord, they should expect that their service would have its ups and downs. Paul spoke of **"many tears and trials,"** of enemies he had and they also would have. He later writes back to them, reminding them that the real enemies are not flesh and blood, but the supernatural principalities and powers of darkness behind human agents (see Eph. 6:12).

Session 2: Counting the cost of discipleship (Acts 20:22-24).

Paul knew his troubles had not ended, but many more awaited him when he would arrive in Jerusalem:

---

*It might come as a surprise to many modern readers to suppose that slaves in first-century Ephesus could have been pastors because our primary paradigm for slavery is African slaves in America. Slavery in the Roman Empire was quite different. S. Scott Bartchy says, "The person in slavery in the first century worked, but his working was not the specific way in which he could be distinguished from the rest of his society." A slave was often "an administrator of funds and personnel and an executive with decision-making power."[9]

22. "And see, now I go bound in the spirit to Jerusalem,
not knowing the things that will happen to me there,
23. except that the Holy Spirit testifies in every city,
saying that chains and tribulations await me."

As he had experienced on many other occasions, Paul had received word from the Holy Spirit that he was to go to Jerusalem. If asked, he could have replied that he was going to Jerusalem because "God told me to." But was this leading of God toward a health, wealth and happiness direction? Obviously not. It was to **chains and tribulations.**

At this point, Paul would have taught the pastors that they must realistically count the cost whenever they accept an assignment to Christian leadership. Pastoring a church is not easy. For all of them will have some price to pay, and for some it will be the ultimate price of life itself. Paul was ready to model this also by saying, **"nor do I count my life dear to myself"** (v. 24).

Session 3: Guarding against counterfeits (Acts 20:25-31).

One quality of Christian leaders is to be able to discern truth from falsehood. The devil will certainly attempt to introduce deception both from without and from within:

29. "For I know this, that after my departure
savage wolves will come in among you,
not sparing the flock.
30. Also from among yourselves men will rise up,
speaking perverse things, to draw away the disciples
after themselves."

The magicians were burning their books and Diana of the Ephesians was on the defensive, so the pastors in Ephesus could expect all manner of attacks, some blatant and some more subtle. As part of the seminar, Paul would have given them instructions on how to deal with such evil infiltrations. The good news is that apparently the pastors learned their lesson well and applied what they knew courageously. The message Jesus gives to the Ephesians many years later, recorded by John in Revelation, says, among other things, "I know your works, your labor, your patience, and that you cannot bear those who are evil. And you have tested those who say they are apostles and are not, and have found them liars" (2:2).

Session 4: Turning the church over to the nationals (Acts 20:32-35).

Many of those who attended Paul's leadership seminar would have been people he had previously trained as church planters in his seminary in Tyrannus's school. He most probably would have taught them what we call today "indigenous church principles," an extremely important missiological concept. Donald McGavran, a renowned missiologist, says, "Stoppage [in church growth] is avoided by using a pattern of church growth that is indefinitely reproducible with the resources available to a given church."[10] Paul indicated that one way he had helped this process was by not loading his personal expenses onto the new churches:

> 33. "I have coveted no one's silver or gold or apparel.
> 34. Yes, you yourselves know that these hands
> have provided for my necessities, and for those
> who were with me."

At the same time, Paul taught that pastors of local churches should be compensated for their services: "Let the elders who rule well be counted worthy of double honor, especially those who labor in the word and in doctrine. For the Scripture says, 'You shall not muzzle an ox while it treads out the grain,' and, 'The laborer is worthy of his wages'" (1 Tim. 5:18).

The Need to Evaluate Prophecy
Acts 21

As Paul continues his trip to Jerusalem, he runs into two incidents in which it seems that prophetic words delivered to him by others might contradict the word he himself had received from the Holy Spirit that he should go to Jerusalem even if **chains and tribulations await [him]** (Acts 20:22). One incident occurs in his stopover in Tyre (see 21:1-6), and the other one during a longer stay in Caesarea (see vv. 7-14).

The incident in Tyre:

> **21:4. And finding disciples, we stayed there seven days. They told Paul through the Spirit not to go up to Jerusalem.**

And the incident in Caesarea:

> **10. And as we stayed many days, a certain prophet named Agabus came down from Judea.**
> **11. When he had come to us, he took Paul's belt, bound his own hands and feet, and said, "Thus says the Holy Spirit, 'So shall the Jews at Jerusalem bind the man who owns this belt, and deliver him into the hands of the Gentiles.'"**
> **12. Now when we heard these things, both we and**

those from that place pleaded with him not to go
up to Jerusalem.

....

In both of these cases, Paul already knew that God had told him to go to Jerusalem, and he also knew he would face serious problems once he arrived there. Yet, words such as these could have been very disturbing to him. Could it be that he had heard from God inaccurately? Could it be that God had changed His mind?

In Tyre, it might have been fairly easy for Paul to judge that the believers could have heard accurately from God about the dangers, and then have allowed their own love for him to shape their advice. Their revelation **through the Spirit** (v. 4) could be explained by Luke's use of the Greek *dia* (through), which could mean "as a consequence of" what the Spirit had told them, as opposed to a similar Greek word *hupo*, which Luke chose not to use and which would have implied that the Holy Spirit was the primary or direct agent of telling Paul not to go.[11]

But the situation in Caesarea with Agabus is a bit more complex. Agabus was a recognized prophet in the churches. Furthermore, he was known to be accurate, as we saw earlier when he prophesied a famine that actually came to pass (see 11:28). Agabus apparently went to Caesarea specifically to bring this prophetic word to Paul.

This prophecy, however, was not all that accurate. Agabus introduced it with a prophetic act that would ordinarily serve to dramatize the event. He prefaced it by saying, **"Thus says the Holy Spirit"** (21:11). And the prophecy itself had two parts:

1. **"So shall the Jews at Jerusalem bind the man who owns this belt"** (v. 11). As it turns out, Paul is bound, but not by Jews; he is bound by Romans (see v. 33).

2. **"So shall the Jews...deliver him into the hands of the**

Gentiles" (v. 11). As it turns out, the Jews have no intention of delivering Paul to the Gentiles, but, rather, they attempt to murder him. The Romans (Gentiles) rescue him *from* the Jews (see vv. 31-33).

How can we explain this prophecy? It would not seem to be sufficient to explain it by arguing that only the *details* might not have been accurate, while the *essence* of Agabus's prophecy was accurate. Wayne Grudem points out, "This explanation does not take full enough account of the fact that these are the *only* two details Agabus mentions—they are, in terms of content, the heart of his prophecy."[12]

Steps Toward Evaluating Personal Prophecy

Christian leaders who believe that the spiritual gifts of the New Testament, such as prophecy, are still actively functioning in the Body of Christ today may often face situations illustrated by Paul and Agabus. I know that I find myself in a similar position many times because, in my role as an international prayer coordinator, I am in close contact with intercessors and prophets who love me and pray for me. One of them is Cindy Jacobs, whose thorough and insightful book *The Voice of God* is scheduled to be released by Regal Books shortly before this volume is released. Meanwhile, here are some useful steps, which I have developed over a period of time, to evaluate personal prophecy:

We cannot take all the words, purportedly from the Holy Spirit, that come our way equally at face value. If we allowed all of them equally to direct our attitudes, our decisions and our actions, we would quickly find ourselves moving in many different directions at the same time, and our leadership effectiveness could thereby be neutralized.

Our decisions and our activities must ultimately be based on what we ourselves sense the Spirit is saying to us, not what He may be say-

ing to others. I like Stanley Horton's comment on the word Paul received from the believers at Tyre: "In other words, because of the prophecy of bonds and imprisonment, the people voiced their feelings that he should not go. But Paul refused to let them force their feelings on him. So he still obeyed what the Holy Spirit directed him personally to do, that is, go on to Jerusalem."[13] If we are true leaders, the buck will stop with us. We will take full personal responsibility before God and before our followers for every decision we make, while being grateful to prayer partners and prophets for their love and concern.

The Holy Spirit, however, does frequently use the prophetic ministry of others to guide us toward our decisions. This is the central value of personal prophecy. How, then, do we know which words we should take seriously and which we should ignore? In my opinion, our starting point must be the character, reputation and gifting of the person who offers the prophecy. Agabus obviously passed this test.

It is also important to keep in mind three distinct steps in receiving a prophetic guidance:

- The *revelation* itself;
- The *interpretation* of the revelation;
- The *application* of the interpretation to real life.

Getting back to the problem Paul had with Agabus. Consider, in light of these three steps, Wayne Grudem's response: "The best solution is to say that Agabus had a '*revelation*' from the Holy Spirit concerning what would happen to Paul in Jerusalem, and gave a prophecy which included his own *interpretation* of this revelation"[14] (italics mine). Having said this, it is clear that Paul himself had to make the final *application*. As in Tyre, he believed that his personal word from the Lord directing him to go to Jerusalem overruled any other opinion that might have come to him through his dear friends and colleagues, gifted as they might be. When he made that known, the others involved appropriately recognized that Paul was correct, and Luke says we ceased [giving Paul advice], saying, "The will of the Lord be done" (21:14).

Three Inherent Limitations

Recognize the inherent limitations of personal prophecy. Bill Hamon, a well-respected prophetic leader, says, "However it may be worded, a personal prophecy will always be partial, progressive and conditional."[15] Prophecies are *partial* because each one touches only a relatively small segment of our lives. Prophecy is *progressive* because it "unfolds and expands gradually over the years, with each prophetic word adding new information and revelation."[16] It is *conditional* because its fulfillment "requires the proper participation and cooperation of the one who receives the prophetic word."[17]

The human factors involved in interpretation and application of personal prophecies can be sifted and tested through agreement. If several responsible people are receiving the same or similar words, the accuracy is more probable.

For several years, I have been keeping what I call a "prophetic journal," which has now reached 29 pages single spaced. In it, I record only certain prophecies directed to my wife, Doris, and me that I have sifted out from many others, believing they merit special consideration in my prayers for direction. Much of what is recorded there could not be made public for a number of reasons. But, as an example of what I am saying, our very important decision to accept the invitation to coordinate the United Prayer Track of the A.D. 2000 and Beyond Movement back in 1991 came largely as a result of many directional prophetic words given to Doris and me through our trusted intercessors.

For example: Before the invitation came, one person had said, "You are now about to face the greatest challenge of your life. It will be a challenge almost beyond belief, but you are to believe the unbelievable." When the invitation came, another person said, "This is not like anything else I've felt. I feel the glory of the Lord around A.D. 2000. Whatever this movement is, get on it! This is a God-ordained program; it is where God is moving right now!" And another one said: "A.D. 2000 is a strong stream of God's movement in these days; you should be a part of it." Still others agreed, and we have now become part of what has truly become the greatest challenge of our ministry careers.

In obedience to the Lord, Paul, likewise, had no choice but to move on to Jerusalem and the Jerusalem jail.

Reflection Questions

1. What do you think of the suggestion that in raising funds for Christian work we might compare what some give to what others give? Can this be abused?

2. When it comes right down to it, how much biblical justification do we have for worshiping on the first day of the week as opposed to keeping the Sabbath?

3. Why would some people doubt that God at times raises dead people to life today just as He did in biblical times?

4. The churches in the first century were all house churches. Do you think it is either unbiblical or unwise to meet in church buildings today?

5. Do you agree that some prophets today hear the voice of God? What are the potential benefits of such ministry? What cautions would you offer?

Notes

1. F. F. Bruce, *The Book of Acts* (Grand Rapids: William B. Eerdmans Publishing Company, 1954; revised edition, 1988), p. 371.
2. William Mitchell Ramsay, *St. Paul the Traveller and the Roman Citizen* (London, England: Hodder & Stoughton, 1925), p. 59.
3. Bruce, *The Book of Acts*, p. 381.
4. Simon J. Kistemaker, *Exposition of the Acts of the Apostles* (Grand Rapids: Baker Book House, 1990), p. 712.
5. Ramsay, *St. Paul the Traveller*, p. 287.
6. Bradley Blue, "Acts and the House Church," *The Book of Acts in Its Graeco-Roman Setting*, ed. David W. J. Gill and Conrad Gempf (Grand Rapids: William B. Eerdmans Publishing Company, 1994), p. 120.
7. Robert Banks, *Paul's Idea of Community* (Peabody, Mass.: Hendrickson Publishers, 1994), p. 32.
8. Ibid., p. 35.
9. S. Scott Bartchy, *First-Century Slavery and 1 Corinthians 7:21* (Missoula, Mont.: The Society of Biblical Literature, 1973), p. 73.
10. Donald A. McGavran, *Understanding Church Growth* (Grand Rapids: William B. Eerdmans Publishing Company, 1970; 1980; third edition revised and edited by C. Peter Wagner, 1990), p. 218.
11. See Stanley M. Horton, *The Book of Acts* (Springfield, Mo.: Gospel Publishing House, 1981), p. 244.
12. Wayne A. Grudem, *The Gift of Prophecy in the New Testament and Today* (Westchester, Ill.: Crossway Books, 1988), p. 97.
13. Horton, *The Book of Acts*, p. 244.
14. Grudem, *The Gift of Prophecy*, p. 100.
15. Bill Hamon, *Prophets and Personal Prophecy* (Destiny Image Publishers, 351 N. Queen Street, Shippensburg, PA 17257, 1987), p. 145.
16. Ibid., p. 147.
17. Ibid., p. 152.

What to Do
with This
Troublemaker?

Paul's last visit to Jerusalem was not the best of experiences. Coming from his high victory of the evangelization of Ephesus and Asia to the jail in Jerusalem was a shocking change. For many other Christian leaders since Paul, however, moving from an extraordinary high to a depressing low has not been unknown. In such situations, looking back to Paul's example of handling his unpleasant experience has been a strong encouragement. Paul managed it splendidly, although this trip to Jerusalem marked the beginning of the end, not only of his active ministry, but of his very life.

We cannot help but wonder why Luke gives so much space in Acts to this experience in Jerusalem. I like the way George Ladd analyzes it: "Luke devotes five and a half chapters to an account of Paul's last visit to Jerusalem. Why does this story merit so much space?" Ladd points out that, unlike what we have seen in

Acts so far, "No new churches were established; no theological or ecclesiastical problems solved. No positive gains came from this visit."[1]

After raising the question, Ladd then goes on to propose an answer: "The importance of these chapters is found in their illustration of Israel's rejection of the Gospel."[2] As we have followed Paul's ministry, we have seen many local incidents of the Jews rejecting the gospel, accompanied by varying degrees of violence. But I think Ladd is right in suggesting that the final rejection must come in Jerusalem, just as the Gospel of Luke places Jesus' final rejection in the same city.

Plans that Didn't Work Out

Paul thought that God was leading him to evangelize Spain, and that Rome would be his base for that mission. By this time, Paul had written his Epistle to the Romans and had stated his goals very clearly. He said, "Whenever I journey to Spain, I shall come to you. For I hope to see you on my journey, and to be helped on my way there by you, if first I may enjoy your company for a while" (15:24). He then told them he was first going to Jerusalem to deliver the offering to the poor Jews that was given by the Gentile believers in Macedonia and Achaia. In light of what is in store for Paul here in Jerusalem, amid many false accusations, it is significant to know his real heart on the crucial matters of Gentile believers and how they relate to Jews. He writes to the Romans: "For if the Gentiles have been partakers of their spiritual things, their duty is also to minister to them in material things" (v. 27). Paul wanted harmony in the Body of Christ.

But this time, Paul's plans did not work out as he wished. He said to the Roman Christians, "When I have performed this and have sealed them this fruit, I shall go by way of you to Spain" (v. 28). Not that he was unaware of the dangers of going to

Jerusalem, even at that time. He had asked the Roman believers for personal intercession: "That you strive together with me in prayers to God for me, that I may be delivered from those in Judea who do not believe, and that my service [the offering] for Jerusalem may be acceptable to the saints" (vv. 30,31). Nevertheless, Paul still expected to "come to [the Romans] with joy by the will of God, and may be refreshed together with you" (v. 32).

Indeed, Paul eventually did go to Rome, but not under the conditions for which he had asked the Romans to pray.

A Welcome and a Warning

21:17. And when we had come to Jerusalem,
the brethren received us gladly.
18. On the following day Paul went in with us to
James, and all the elders were present.
19. When he had greeted them, he told in detail
those things which God had done among the
Gentiles through his ministry.
20. And when they heard it, they glorified the Lord....

This was Paul's welcome to Jerusalem by the church leaders there. It was cordial, and well it should have been. Paul brought with him what must have been a substantial monetary gift from the Gentile churches to help the poor believers in Jerusalem. It seems a bit strange that Luke doesn't mention this, although he refers to it later when he tells of Paul's defense before Festus, and Paul says, "Now after many years I came to bring alms and offerings to my nation" (24:17).

As this scenario unfolds, we need to keep in mind that Paul, although he himself was a full-blooded Jew who could trace his genealogy back to Abraham with the best of them, must have been quite thin on patience with his fellow Jews by this time. He had just barely escaped with his life from the Jews in Corinth. Other Jews had driven him out of Berea and Thessalonica. They had attacked him in Antioch of Pisidia, in Iconium, and incited a mob to stone him to death in Lystra. His attitude toward Jews could not have been the most positive.

But it was a two-way street. The attitude of the Jews, including some of the Jewish believers, was not that positive toward Paul either. At least from the way Luke tells the story, the Jerusalem elders moved Paul quickly from his agenda of praising God for blessings on the Gentiles to their own agenda without so much as a transition:

> **21:20. ...And they said to him, "You see, brother, how many myriads of Jews there are who have believed, and they are all zealous for the law."**

The elders' warning to Paul begins here. The issue is keeping the law of Moses. Because of the Jerusalem Council about eight years prior to this, the question of *Gentiles* obeying the law was no longer being raised (see v. 25). Nor was there a problem with the Messianic Jews in Jerusalem who were still keeping the law as they were expected to do. But how about the minority Jews in the majority Gentile churches Paul had been planting? Here is the thorny issue:

> **21. "but they have been informed about you that you teach all the Jews who are among the Gentiles to forsake Moses, saying that they ought not to circumcise**

their children nor walk according to their customs."

....

Paul found himself being accused of teaching Jews to stop following the Jewish law. This in all probability blindsided him, for such teaching, as we see clearly in his Epistles, was not part of the way he actually believed or taught. As is all too frequently the case, however, a false accusation, blown out of proportion and propagated by enemies of the gospel, can be devastating. The orthodox Jewish mentality contains no categories to assimilate the statement from a Jew like Paul that "I have become all things to all men, that I might by all means save some" (1 Cor. 9:22). This may be simple enough for us Gentiles to say, but for Paul, his commitment to the principle set him on the road ultimately leading to his death.

As a stopgap, the church elders persuaded Paul to attempt to diffuse the criticism by identifying with some Jewish believers who were fulfilling a Nazirite vow like the one Paul took toward the end of his first visit to Corinth. He did so (see Acts 21:23,24,26), but not to much avail.

The crisis came when some Jews from Asia, probably Ephesus, spotted this missionary whom they had learned to hate in the Jewish Temple. They undoubtedly thought they might be able to get away with some things here in Jerusalem that they would not have dared to attempt in Ephesus, so they captured Paul, accused him falsely and illegally commenced to beat him to death. At that moment, the Roman authorities stepped into the picture, rescued Paul from his attackers just in time and took him into protective custody.

Paul had arrived at the Jerusalem jail!

Paul on the Defensive

Instead of going right to Rome as he had planned, Paul was

forced to spend no less than two years in Jerusalem and in nearby Caesarea explaining himself, his ministry, his theology and his
patriotism to both Jews and Gentiles. As a preliminary overview,
here are the five major incidents recorded by Luke throughout
this lengthy episode. How many other such incidents took place
and Luke did not record, if any, we do not know.

1. Paul lets a hostile Jewish crowd in Jerusalem know who
    he is and why he went to minister to Gentiles in the first
    place (see 21:37—22:23).
2. Paul meets with the Jewish Sanhedrin to address their
    concerns (see 22:30—23:11). He is then escorted to
    Caesarea.
3. In Caesarea, the Roman governor, Felix, calls a court ses-
    sion and Paul's accusers come from Jerusalem (see
    23:34—24:27).
4. Felix's successor, Governor Festus, calls a similar court
    session, again with Jewish accusers from Jerusalem (see
    25:1-12).
5. When Festus's friend King Agrippa comes to Caesarea to
    visit, they invite Paul in to state his position once again
    (see 25:13—26:32).

Why Were the Jews So Vitriolic?

The Roman commander who sent soldiers to rescue Paul was
named Claudius Lysias (see 23:26). Fortunately, he turns out to
be a fair and just military officer. He at first thought Paul was one
of the fugitives from justice for whom his agents had been search-
ing, but after this was straightened out and Paul's true identity
was established, Lysias granted Paul's request to address the mob
of Jews who had been trying to murder him.

The unruly crowd calmed down somewhat when Paul switched from the Greek language he had been speaking to Claudius Lysias to Aramaic ("Hebrew" in *The New King James Version*), which was the first language of this crowd of Jerusalem Jews. He started by saying:

22:1. "Brethren and fathers, hear my defense before you now."

It is important to remember that Paul's audience here would have included Messianic Jewish believers as well as unbelieving Jews. This is not to imply that the believers among them would have been participating in the effort to beat Paul to death, but it is worthy of note that they did not overtly oppose the effort either. Why?

Perhaps they were too few to have any influence, although the elders had just told Paul **how many myriads of Jews there are who have believed** (21:20). No one really knows exactly how many believers were in Jerusalem at that time or what percentage of the population they might have been. But it must have been quite significant, considering that at least 5,000 Jewish male believers were there 25 years prior to this time (see 4:4), with the total probably nearer 15,000. Some have ventured to estimate that the number by this time might have been approaching 100,000, although naturally they wouldn't all have been in the city of Jerusalem.

If, in fact, a large number of believers were in Jerusalem at this time, their failure to defend Paul in any known or effective way could possibly indicate that they were unwilling to take a public stand on the validity of Paul's missionary work to the Gentiles. Although they would undoubtedly maintain their formal theological agreement with the Jerusalem Council when meeting alone with Paul (see 21:25), it could well be that in a public forum like this, they found themselves facing a battle they did not want to fight with their nonbelieving Jewish friends and relatives.

It could have been that the believers' identity as Messianic Jews was more important to some of them than their unity with the non-Jewish segments of the Body of Christ. By this time, they could have come to value their peaceful social relationships with other Jews in the city very highly, perhaps too highly. It is not unusual now, and would not have been unusual then, for a Christian community, over a span of 25 years, to accommodate to the culture around it so much that it forfeit some of the sharp edges of its theological commitments to maintain comfort.

A. J. Mattill Jr., is quite blunt about this matter when he writes, "The Jerusalem church knew that if it declared its solidarity with Paul [by doing certain things], it would destroy the possibility of its own mission among the Jews, indeed, would risk its own destruction at the hands of Jews who could not tolerate any preaching of freedom from the Law."[3]

The patience of the Jews came to an end when Paul, in telling of his experience with Jesus on the Damascus road, said:

22:21. "Then [Jesus] said to me, 'Depart, for
I will send you far from here to the Gentiles.'"
22. And they listened to him until this word, and then
they raised their voices and said, "Away with such a fellow from the earth, for he is not fit to live!"
23. Then, as they cried out and tore off their
clothes and threw dust into the air,
24. the commander ordered him to be brought
into the barracks,...

Can Christians Be Racist?

It is safe to assume that those who were calling for Paul's execution were the unbelieving Jews in the crowd. They, of course, had never agreed to the findings of the Council of Jerusalem; indeed, they in all probability knew nothing about it. What exactly was the issue that so infuriated them? I like the way John Stott says it: "In their eyes proselytism (making Gentiles into Jews) was fine; but evangelism (making Gentiles into Christians without first making them Jews) was an abomination." Now notice very carefully Stott's next phrase, which goes below the surface to the heart of the matter: "It was tantamount to saying that Jews and Gentiles were equal, for they both needed to come to God through Christ, and that on identical terms."[4]

Another way of putting this is that the Jews in Jerusalem at that time were quite racist. They considered their own race superior to non-Jews. Even slaves, the lowest rung on the social ladder, who were Gentiles would be forced by their Jewish masters to become Jews. Joachim Jeremias says, "Gentile slaves of both sexes who became the property of a Jew were made to accept baptism....If the slave were a woman this baptism signified *conversion to Judaism*; male slaves had to complete this conversion by submitting to circumcision" [italics his].[5]

The question that naturally comes to our minds is: How about the Christians, or Messianic Jews as they were called in Jerusalem? Wouldn't they be different from the others? We would wish the answer was yes. But suppose we ask the same question about ourselves—let's say those of us who are white Christians in America today? Does being Christians exempt us from participating in what is clearly the number one national American sin: racism? After studying this issue for some time, my reluctant conclusion is no, Christians are not exempt from racism, I'm ashamed to say, because I am one of them. I would hope that the fruit of the Holy Spirit enables us to handle our inbred racism with a bit more grace than some of our non-Christian counterparts, but that does not exonerate us from our share of the national sin, nor excuse us from taking concrete and positive steps toward meaningful repentance and reconciliation.

Having admitted that, we can look back on the believers in Jerusalem without a holier-than-thou attitude. Here was the apostle Paul, whom we revere as perhaps the Christian leader second in importance only to Jesus, being beaten with the intent to kill on the streets of Jerusalem. And as Mattill puts it, "But where were the Jewish Christians? They could have helped because of their faithfulness to the Law and the Temple, but they sat idly by."[6] Paul's body had been saved by the Roman soldiers, but his spirit must have been devastated.

Citizenship Has Its Advantages

The Roman commander, Claudius Lysias, was both surprised and perplexed at what was happening. He wanted to find out the truth from Paul, so he ordered a centurion to tie Paul and beat him thoroughly before the interrogation. This was not an unusual way to treat suspects in those days, except for Roman citizens. Knowing this:

> 25. ...Paul said to the centurion who stood by,
> "Is it lawful for you to scourge a man who is a
> Roman, and uncondemned?"
> 26. When the centurion heard that, he went and
> told the commander, saying, "Take care what you do,
> for this man is a Roman."
> 29. Then immediately those who were about to examine
> him withdrew from him; and the commander was also

afraid after he found out that he was a Roman, and
because he had bound him.

We may wonder why Paul claimed his Roman citizenship
here, while he and Silas did not do so when they were being
flogged before going to jail in Philippi. A likely explanation is
that in Philippi a close personal bond existed between the members of the nucleus of the new church and Paul, who had led most
of them to Christ. Paul probably thought that using his citizenship credential to avoid physical persecution would be a bad role
model for fellow Christians who did not enjoy such citizenship.
But Jerusalem was not Philippi! At this point, as we have seen,
Paul's personal relationship with the local believers was not all
that cordial, and claiming an exemption from scourging would
have little or no direct influence on the local Christian or
Messianic community.

Furthermore, Paul was not characterized by a martyr complex.
As a reading of 2 Corinthians 11 will confirm, he had suffered
more than his share of physical and emotional crises in his ministry. He had known prophetically before coming to Jerusalem
that trouble was in store for him, and in contemplating that he
said, "nor do I count my life dear to myself" (Acts 20:24).
Nevertheless, he did not consider suffering a desirable thing
when it could legitimately be avoided. So he did what was necessary to avoid it. Roman citizenship had its advantages.

Divide and Conquer

22:30. The next day, because he wanted to know for certain why he was accused by the Jews, he [the commander]
released him from his bonds, and commanded the chief

> priests and all their council to appear, and brought Paul
> down and set him before them.

When Claudius Lysias realized that he was not going to get the information he wanted by beating and interrogating Paul, he went to Plan B and called the Jewish Sanhedrin into session. The Sanhedrin was meeting in the same room where it had heard Stephen's argument more than 20 years earlier, and where, in all likelihood, Paul himself had participated in council deliberations as a member of the Sanhedrin. As we may recall, Stephen first raised the issues about whether people could be saved apart from the Jewish law and the Jewish Temple, and he ultimately gave his life for his radical ideas. What has changed? Here is Paul standing in exactly the same place with the Jewish leaders wanting to add him to the honor roll of Christian martyrs. It was the same issue, the sin of racism being at the root.

From time to time, it is good for us to remember that even the greatest heroes of the faith are human beings and they are susceptible to the same temptations and sins the rest of us have. As a part of this meeting with the Sanhedrin, the high priest, Ananias, and Paul get into a personal tiff, and Paul loses his cool:

> 23:3. Then Paul said to him, "God will strike you,
> you whitewashed wall! For you sit to judge me
> according to the law, and do you command me to
> be struck contrary to the law?"

This would not have been a good thing to say to anyone, much less the high priest. But Paul then did the right thing. As soon as it was brought to his attention, he admitted his impropriety and apologized (see vv. 4,5).

Paul was a Pharisee, and probably a member of the Sanhedrin itself at one time. But whether he had been or not, he knew well that the Pharisees were a strong minority in the Sanhedrin, serving alongside the majority Sadducees. He also knew that, although they were both Jews, they had sensitive doctrinal differences. The Sadducees were similar to what we would today call "theological liberals" because they denied, among other things, the resurrection of the dead and the reality of the spirit world. Whether he had premeditated it or not we are unsure, but Paul skillfully connected his viewpoint to the resurrection of the dead and, thereby, set the Pharisees and Sadducees off on a theological debate. He had decided to divide and conquer.

For some of the Pharisees, winning their argument against the Sadducees suddenly became more important than condemning Paul, and they said:

> 9. "We find no evil in this man; but if a spirit or an angel has spoken to him, let us not fight against God."

The battle heated up so much that for the third time the Roman soldiers rescued Paul:

> 10. Now when there arose a great dissension, the commander, fearing lest Paul might be pulled to pieces by them, commanded the soldiers to go down and take him by force from among them, and bring him into the barracks.

As Paul went from incident to incident, he must have felt

more and more discouraged. He still had his life, although his body would have been severely bruised and painful from the beating the Jews had given him before the soldiers stepped in. His plans of warm fellowship with the believers in Jerusalem, followed by a positive send-off to Rome and Spain, had by then vaporized. Remembering that his chains and imprisonment had been prophesied before coming to Jerusalem would have been little consolation. In the midst of all this, Jesus did a wonderful thing. He appeared to Paul personally!

Jesus Appears

> 11. But the following night the Lord stood by him and said, "Be of good cheer, Paul; for as you have testified for Me in Jerusalem, so you must also bear witness at Rome."

This is just what Paul needed most to regain the physical, emotional and spiritual fortitude he would need to carry him through the rest of this trying experience. This was not the only time Jesus had appeared to Paul since his personal introduction to Him on the Damascus road. When Paul returned to Jerusalem after his conversion and was in danger again of being captured by the Jews, Jesus had appeared and warned him to leave (see 22:18). In Corinth, when the Jews there were taking Paul to Gallio's court, Jesus appeared to him in a vision and told him he would not be harmed (see 18:9,10). Most probably other incidents occurred that Luke does not record.

Interestingly, some people doubt that the spiritual gift of apostle could still be in operation today. One of the arguments purports that one of the requirements for being an apostle is supposedly to have seen Jesus in person (based precariously on Acts

1:21,22), so we could not have any more apostles because Jesus is now in heaven. But Paul was certainly an apostle, and he bases that office, among other things, on having seen Jesus (see 1 Cor. 9:1). Paul, however, never saw Jesus in person during His earthly ministry. The Jesus Paul saw, then, must have been the risen Christ who came and appeared to him personally, as in the incidents just mentioned. If this is true, there is therefore no theological reason why Jesus couldn't or wouldn't do the same thing in other times and at other places. Although such a thing has not happened to me personally, some trusted friends of mine have given me their word that it has happened to them.

This by itself, of course, does not qualify each person who ever sees Jesus to claim to be an apostle. To me, the notion that seeing Jesus personally would be a nonnegotiable prerequisite for receiving the gift of apostle is not a good argument, but even if it was, it would not neutralize the possibility of true apostles serving the Church today. Although we do not always use the name, I believe the function and the office of apostle have always been with the Church through the ages.

Angry Jews on a Hunger Strike

23:12. And when it was day, some of the Jews banded together and bound themselves under an oath, saying that they would neither eat nor drink till they had killed Paul. 13. Now there were more than forty who had formed this conspiracy.

Paul leaves Jerusalem and ends up in Caesarea because the plans of the Jews to kill him, rather than subside, only gain momentum. The oath of a hunger strike by most of the radical Jews signaled to the Romans that if they were going to protect Paul and give him a decent trial, they had better get him out of Jerusalem to a safer place.

Claudius Lysias, the military commander, did a wise thing. He put together a large detachment of foot soldiers and cavalry, which escorted Paul to Caesarea where the Roman governor, Felix, lived and worked. Lysias sent a letter along, explaining the situation, but notably without a formal accusation. By rights, Felix should, therefore, have released Paul, but he didn't want to risk the Jews being upset with him. So he gave Paul comfortable accommodations in the palace Herod the Great had built, and where Felix himself also had his residence.

Paul's First Real Trial

We mentioned earlier that Paul had to defend himself in public five separate times during these two years in Jerusalem and Caesarea. It might be stretching it to describe his appearance before the Sanhedrin as a legitimate trial, so this event with Felix could be considered the first trial.

> **24:1.** Now after five days Ananias the high priest came down with the elders and a certain orator [attorney] named Tertullus. These gave evidence to the governor against Paul.

Three accusations were brought against Paul, and he responded to all three. Let's look at them:

Accusation Number One

> **5.** "For we have found this man a plague, a creator of dis-

sension among all the Jews throughout the world,..."

Felix would have paid close attention to this accusation because the Roman government was constantly on the vigil to detect any kind of political unrest or uprisings that may be occurring. Another translation of "plague" could be "troublemaker," and I have introduced this word in the title of this chapter, "What to Do with This Troublemaker?" Tertullus, the attorney, wanted Felix to see Paul as a potentially dangerous political revolutionary.

Response Number One

> 11. "because you may ascertain that it is no more than twelve days since I went up to Jerusalem to worship.
> 12. And they neither found me in the temple disputing with anyone nor inciting the crowd, either in the synagogues or in the city.
> 13. Nor can they prove the things of which they now accuse me."

Paul's major achievement here was to put his accusers on the spot in court, challenging them to produce witnesses to verify that he was responsible for stirring up a disturbance in Jerusalem during the last 12 days. They must have been embarrassed when they could not provide these witnesses.

Accusation Number Two

> 5. "...[Paul is] a ringleader of the sect of the Nazarenes."

We should keep in mind that the word "Christian" at this time was being used only for Gentile believers. Messianic Jews back then, and even some today, prefer to avoid the term for themselves. This is the only time believers were called "Nazarenes" in Scripture. It sounds fairly natural to us today, however, considering the worldwide spread of the Church of the Nazarene, which is headquartered in Kansas City, Missouri.

The legal tactic Tertullus was using here was to try to cast the Nazarenes into the mold of a *political* movement that Felix might see as a danger to the public welfare. He may not have known that Felix was well informed about Christianity, also known as "the Way" (see v. 22).

Response Number Two

14. "But this I confess to you, that according to the Way which they call a sect, so I worship the God of my fathers, believing all things which are written in the Law and in the Prophets."

Paul definitely testified that he was a Christian. But he went on from there to affirm, as Gallio also had concluded in Corinth, that **"the Way"** was not a political party, but rather a fulfillment of Judaism itself, in which it was firmly rooted.

Accusation Number Three

6. "He even tried to profane the temple,..."

The Romans had given the Jews, as a *religio licita*, a legal religion—jurisdiction of the internal affairs in their Temple. If they could prove that Paul had tried to desecrate the Temple, Paul would have been in serious trouble.

Response Number Three

17. "Now after many years I came to bring alms
and offerings to my nation,
18. in the midst of which some Jews from Asia
found me purified in the temple, neither with
a mob nor with tumult.
19. They ought to have been here before you to object if
they had anything against me."

Instead of desecrating the Temple, they did just the opposite. Paul had entered the Temple to purify himself, thus affirming his own personal commitment to temple worship and to the God of the Jews. His reason for coming to Jerusalem was to bless the Jewish people. If the Asian Jews had an accusation, according to Roman law, they would have to be present in person to press charges.

The upshot of the trial was not a "hung jury" but a "hung governor," so to speak. He had no grounds on which to accuse Paul, but at the same time he did not want to offend the Jews. So he postponed a final decision instead of releasing Paul as he should have done.

A Rerun for Governor Festus

27. But after two years Porcius Festus succeeded Felix;
and Felix, wanting to do the Jews a favor, left Paul bound.

When Festus took office as the governor, he personally went to Jerusalem for a briefing on Paul's case, then held a trial in Caesarea similar to that of Felix's trial. The upshot of this trial was that Festus wanted to take Paul back to Jerusalem to face the Sanhedrin. Paul was not foolish. He was aware that going to Jerusalem would in all probability end his life, so he decided to go over Festus's head and appeal to Caesar:

> 25:10. So Paul said, "I stand at Caesar's judgment seat, where I ought to be judged. To the Jews I have done no wrong, as you very well know.
> 11. ...I appeal to Caesar."
> 12. Then Festus, when he had conferred with the council, answered, "You have appealed to Caesar? To Caesar you shall go!"

If nothing else, Paul now had his ticket to Rome!

Satisfying Agrippa's Curiosity

> 13. And after some days King Agrippa and Bernice came to Caesarea to greet Festus.
> 14. When they had been there many days, Festus laid Paul's case before the king,...
> 22. Then Agrippa said to Festus, "I also would like to hear the man myself." "Tomorrow," he said, "you shall hear him."

Agrippa, great-grandson of the notorious Herod the Great, was a Jew and had considerable influence among the Jewish community. More out of curiosity than anything else, he requests that Paul be brought in for a hearing. This was not as much a trial, having the accusers present, as an assembly called together to listen to Paul's account of what had been happening.

The details of this hearing add little to what we have already discussed in other places. Paul relates what is the third account of his conversion on the Damascus road in the book of Acts, and in it he emphasizes his call to evangelize the Gentiles and **"to open their eyes, in order to turn them from darkness to light, and from the power of Satan to God"** (26:18).

The passage also includes the much-preached verse:

26:28. Then Agrippa said to Paul, "You almost persuade me to become a Christian."

Not to ruin any sermons, but biblical scholars believe that a more accurate version of what Agrippa was really saying to Paul was, "In a short time you are trying to persuade me to act as a Christian."[7]

Paul never lost his evangelistic passion, even when finishing his fifth public defense against false charges. His reply to Agrippa is classic:

29. And Paul said, "I would to God that not only you, but also all who hear me today, might become both almost and altogether such as I am, except for these chains."

Both Festus and Agrippa agreed that Paul was innocent and that if he had not appealed to Caesar he could have gone free. But, as we know, it was God's will that Paul go to Rome, and even if the conditions were not what he would have wished, he was ready for the trip.

Reflection Questions

1. The end of Acts depicts very graphically the Jewish rejection of the gospel. What is the state of affairs today? Do you think this will change?
2. Why did the Jewish believers in Jerusalem seem to give Paul a warm welcome and then begin to quarrel with him? Why didn't they take Paul's side when he was arrested?
3 Review the section under "Can Christians Be Racist?" Express your own feelings not only about the first century, but also about the twentieth century.
4. When Paul was at a personal low point, Jesus appeared to him in person. Have you ever heard of something like that happening to someone you know?
5. Why wasn't the word "Christian" being applied to Jewish believers in Paul's day? What do you think is the preference of Jewish believers today?

Notes

1. George Eldon Ladd, *The Young Church: Acts of the Apostles* (Nashville: Abingdon Press, 1964), p. 78.
2. Ibid., p. 79.
3. A. J. Mattill Jr., "The Purpose of Acts: Schneckenburger Reconsidered," *Apostolic History and the Gospel*, ed. W. Ward Gasque and Ralph P. Martin (Grand Rapids: William B. Eerdmans Publishing Company, 1970), p. 116.
4. John Stott, *The Spirit, the Church and the World: The Message of Acts* (Downers Grove, Ill.: InterVarsity Press, 1990), p. 348.

5. Joachim Jeremias, *Jerusalem in the Time of Jesus* (Philadelphia, Pa.: Fortress Press, 1969), p. 348.

6. Mattill, "The Purpose of Acts," *Apostolic History and the Gospel*, p. 116.

7. See Simon J. Kistemaker, *Exposition of the Acts of the Apostles* (Grand Rapids: Baker Book House, 1990), p. 906.

CHAPTER

8

Acts 27 and 28

Destination: Rome

Paul's desire to go to Rome, set back measurably by his imprisonment, would not have been primarily to introduce the gospel, evangelize and plant churches, as he had done in many other cities. Someone else had been the pioneer church planter in Rome, for Christianity was by then already solidly established in the capital of the Roman Empire.

Christianity in Rome

How many house churches might have been located in Rome by this time we have no way of knowing exactly, but likely quite a few. In the Epistle Paul had written to these Roman believers a few years previously, he mentioned some house churches by name. For example, Priscilla and Aquila, who had shared their tentmaking business with Paul in Corinth and Ephesus, had by then returned to Rome and hosted a church in their home (see

Rom. 16:3-5). He also mentions the "household of Aristobulus" and the "household of Narcissus," which may also indicate house churches (see vv. 10,11). Then Paul speaks of the "brethren who are with" Asyncritus, Phlegon, Hermas, Patrobas and Hermes, possibly a unit of its own (see v. 14), and others as well.

The Roman Christians, largely, it would seem, because of their strategic location in the capital city, had such a powerful testimony that Paul could say, "I thank my God through Jesus Christ for you all, that your faith is spoken of throughout the whole world" (1:8). If all roads led to Rome, then all roads would also lead out of Rome, and the gospel could and did spread along them.

It is true that Paul had expressed to them his desire to "have some fruit among you" (v. 13). He had also said, "I am ready to preach the gospel to you who are in Rome" (v. 15). But these statements could easily be understood as expressing a vision for ministry to believers as well as evangelistic ministry to unbelievers. Paul, as a pioneer missionary, would minister to believers as the need presented itself, but not as his career goal. I mention this because later in the same letter Paul said to the Romans, "And so I have made it my aim to preach the gospel, not where Christ was named, lest I should build on another man's foundation" (15:20). Clearly, someone else had already laid the foundation in Rome.

Athens, as we have seen, was known far and wide for its idolatry and philosophy; Corinth was known for its immorality and wealth, and Ephesus was known for its magic. Rome, in turn, was known for its extraordinary political power over a large part of the world. John Stott gives us a vivid summary of the political accomplishments of Rome: "It treated its conquered subjects and their religions with comparatively humane tolerance; it somehow managed to integrate Romans, Greeks, Jews and 'Barbarians' into its social life; it protected the Greek culture and language; it inculcated respect for the rule of law; it gained a reputation for efficient administration and postal communication; and it facili-tated travel by its ambitious system of roads and ports, policed by its legions and its navy, so preserving for the benefit of all the long-standing *pax romana.*"[1] Certainly the hand of God must have been behind the government of Rome to prepare the way for sending His Son, Jesus, so that the message of salvation could spread rapidly.

Roman justice allowed Paul to escape with his life from the Jews at Jerusalem, and the Roman transportation system was ready to carry him, this time by sea, to the capital city.

Luke Ships Out with Paul

27:1. And when it was decided that we should sail to Italy, they delivered Paul and some other prisoners to one named Julius, a centurion of the Augustan Regiment.
2. So, entering a ship of Adramyttium, we put to sea, meaning to sail along the coasts of Asia. Aristarchus, a Macedonian of Thessalonica, was with us.

Luke begins this episode with the statement: **And when it was decided that we should sail to Italy.** The **we** means that Luke was again with Paul. The last time Luke used "we" was after arriv-ing in Jerusalem, but before Paul had his meeting with the elders of the Jerusalem church. Luke does not indicate that he was with Paul during all the trouble with the Jews in Jerusalem, leading to his rescue by the Roman authorities, and the two years as a pris-oner in Herod's Palace in Caesarea. Some scholars speculate that Luke could have remained in the Caesarea area doing research for his two-volume work, which we now know as Luke and Acts.

It also could have been that he spent a good part of that time back home in Philippi. Whatever the case may be, Luke was with Paul once again when the time came to sail to Rome.

How would Luke have secured passage on this ship among the prisoners who were being taken to Rome? The vessel evidently was one of those huge grain freighters that regularly carried wheat to Rome from Egypt, the so-called breadbasket of the Roman Empire. Some biblical scholars speculate that Luke, as well as Aristarchus from Thessalonica, posed as slaves owned by Paul and thus were allowed to go along with him to care for his needs. Others say that Luke may have hired on as the ship's physician. Perhaps an even more likely assumption could be that such a large ship would not necessarily limit the number of passengers it carried to a group of Roman prisoners, but could also have accommodated others who simply booked passage and paid their respective fares.

Who were the other prisoners? I think William Ramsay helps us by pointing out that they were undoubtedly quite different from Paul, who was "a man of distinction, a Roman citizen who had appealed for trial to the supreme court in Rome."[2] And the other prisoners? "[They] had been in all probability already condemned to death, and were going to supply the perpetual demand which Rome made on the provinces for human victims to amuse the populace by their death in the arena."[3]

This observation also serves as a reminder to us that the Rome to which Paul was headed may have been a brilliant political phenomenon, but it had its dark side as well. A populace that would consider watching fellow human beings suffer cruel and traumatic deaths as a primary spectator attraction in its public stadiums must have been influenced, more than most, by powerful spirits of violence. This undoubtedly would have ominous ramifications throughout society as a whole.

Paul's First Word for the Ship's Officers

....

27:9. Now when much time had been spent, and
sailing was now dangerous...Paul advised them,
10. saying, "Men, I perceive that this voyage will
end with disaster and much loss, not only of the
cargo and ship, but also our lives."

....

Winter was approaching rapidly, and with it the notorious stormy
weather in that part of the Mediterranean Sea. The officers of
the ship were well aware of this when they harbored to survive
one of the early storms in a place called Fair Havens, on the
southern shores of the Island of Crete. The officers, however,
wanted to take the risk of pushing ahead a bit farther to the port
of Phoenix. If they had to spend their winter on land, they were
anxious to move on to a more luxuriously equipped harbor.

Paul, however, knew that this was a poor decision and that it
would end in disaster for them all. Where did Paul get this information? He could have drawn on the human experience he had
accumulated by sailing frequently on ships in and around the
Mediterranean Sea, and this is the most common interpretation
in the commentaries I am following. It does seem odd, however,
that Paul, who was a tentmaker, not a sailor, by trade would have
matched his nautical wisdom against that of professional sailors
who had spent most of their lives at sea. It would be similar to my
daring to offer technical advice to a commercial airline pilot
because I travel 100,000 miles a year in the air.

Another more reasonable possibility is that Paul had received
a prophetic word from God concerning this trip. After they
pushed off and the problems Paul warned against had begun, Paul
then received a second word, this one specifically attributed to a

voice from God through an angel. If Paul's second word was clearly supernatural, it does not seem farfetched to suppose the first one could also have been supernatural.

There is no reason to expect that a ship's crew of unbelievers would have any inclination to attach some sort of divine directive to the advice of a landlubber passenger. If the crew had been believers, however, one might have had other expectations. And in those days, when the prophetic ministry was much better understood than it is in many places today, a believing crew might well have put aside its professional expertise and listened to the word from God through the apostle. I mention this because, unfortunately, in all too many of our churches today, such prophetic words are not given due credibility, and the consequences of substituting technical know-how for God's direction are similar. Unfortunately, many church leaders would take an approach similar to what the sailors took:

11. Nevertheless the centurion was more persuaded
by the helmsman and the owner of the ship than
by the things spoken by Paul.
12. And because the harbor was not suitable to winter
in, the majority advised to set sail from there...

The word **majority** can be misleading. Although those of us who live in a democratic society know that the majority can be, and often is, wrong, we frequently insist on making important decisions in our churches on the basis of 51 percent or more of the votes. This is especially unwise when God Himself is trying to say something to the Church contrary to the opinion of most, as He evidently was on the ship on which Paul was sailing. Fortunately, Christianity worldwide seems to be moving strongly toward a more biblical view of basing church decisions on the Word of God rather than on the wisdom of professionals, when there is a choice. This is not to imply that the wisdom of professionals in our churches is not important. Indeed, most day-to-day decisions are made through consecrated human wisdom, taking into account the way the majority feels about an issue. I believe, however, that churches, like sailors, should be prepared for the exception to the rule when a divine word contrary to the majority opinion comes through a servant of God, such as the apostle Paul, or from those who have a recognized prophetic ministry today.

The Storm and Paul's Second Word

This story reminds me of Jonah. Jonah also ignored a word from God, and to get his attention, God placed him in the midst of a life-threatening storm at sea. It worked in the case of Jonah, and it also worked on the good ship Adramyttium.

14. ...a tempestuous head wind arose, called Euroclydon.
18. ...we were exceedingly tempest-tossed,...
20. Now when neither sun nor stars appeared for many days, and no small tempest beat on us, all hope that we would be saved was finally given up.

The professional sailors were now willing to listen to Paul. Their hope was gone! And this time Paul is more specific in indicating that his prophetic word comes directly from God.

21. ...Paul stood in the midst of them and said, "Men, you should have listened to me, and not have sailed from Crete and incurred this disaster and loss.
22. And now I urge you to take heart, for there will be no

loss of life among you, but only of the ship.
23. For there stood by me this night an angel of the God
to whom I belong and whom I serve,
24. saying, 'Do not be afraid, Paul; you must be
brought before Caesar; and indeed God has granted
you all those who sail with you.'
25. Therefore take heart, men, for I believe God that it
will be just as it was told me.
26. However, we must run aground on a certain island."

One thing many will notice about this second prophecy is that it differs from the first at a key point. In the first prophecy, Paul said that if they sailed from Fair Haven they would lose their lives. This time, he says their lives will be spared. One way this could be explained is to suppose, as many do, that the first word was not prophetic at all, but simply human advice. This is possible, but I lean toward seeing them both as prophetic. How, then, would I explain it?

A Conditional Prophecy

Some may recall that in chapter 6, when I discussed the need to evaluate prophecies such as Paul was receiving on his way to Jerusalem, I said we should keep in mind that personal prophecies are (1) partial, (2) progressive, and (3) conditional. A reasonable explanation of this event, then, is to postulate that the first word Paul had received about all the passengers losing their lives if the ship had sailed was conditional. We are not told explicitly what the conditions might have been. But those who have had experience in prophetic ministries and who have monitored the way prophecies are ordinarily fulfilled report that a frequent condition, if not the most frequent, is prayer. Brother

Andrew, for example, has written an excellent book on intercessory prayer, which has the striking title *And God Changed His Mind* (Chosen Books), emphasizing this idea.

Theologically speaking, a sovereign God is never double minded. But the sovereign God, for reasons that obviously please Him, has designed His world so that certain things happen in history contingent on decisions and actions of human beings. He changed His mind about destroying Ninevah in Jonah's time, for example, when Ninevah repented. Here, I believe, Paul was instrumental in fulfilling a condition that allowed his fellow passengers, in this case 276 of them (see 27:37), to live through the shipwreck rather than die.

This condition, I strongly suspect, was intercessory prayer. For one thing, the power of intercessory prayer is much more awesome than we often think, as I argue in my book *Prayer Shield* (Regal Books). For another thing, consider the words the angel spoke to Paul: "'indeed God has granted you all those who sail with you'" (v. 24). Clearly, the statement that God had "'granted'" the lives of the fellow passengers to Paul could best be understood by supposing that Paul had indeed asked God for them. Otherwise it is difficult to explain. These other prisoners, for example, were not, nor ever would be, Paul's in any literal sense of the word. Whether any were ever converted, we have no way of knowing except that Luke is usually inclined to mention conversions in his narrative when they do occur. It seems likely that Paul, having compassion characteristic of the fruit of the Spirit, had asked for God's mercy on them all, and received it. History belongs to the intercessors, as Walter Wink might say.

The Shipwreck

....

41. But striking a place where two seas met, they ran the

> ship aground; and the prow stuck fast and remained
> immovable, but the stern was being broken up by
> the violence of the waves.
> 43. But the centurion,...commanded that those who could
> swim should jump overboard first and get to land,
> 44. and the rest, some on boards and some on parts of the
> ship. And so it was that they all escaped safely to land.

The prophecy is fulfilled! Not only did the passengers survive the shipwreck itself, but one more thing. Those who were prisoners could easily have been killed by their guards! According to Roman custom, if prisoners escaped, their guards would have been subject to receive their allotted punishment, in this case, possibly thrown to the lions in the Coliseum. But the centurion put a stop to that in deference to his most distinguished prisoner, the apostle Paul, and their lives had been spared from not one, but two potential causes of death through Paul's prayers.

Miracles on Malta

> 28:1. Now when they had escaped, they then found out
> that the island was called Malta.
> 2. And the natives showed an unusual kindness; for they
> kindled a fire and made us all welcome, because of the
> rain that was falling and because of the cold.

Back in those days, it would not be unusual for the occupants of a wrecked ship to be taken as slaves by those who lived on the land. But in this case, perhaps because of the presence of the Roman centurion and his soldiers, they showed warm hospitality instead.

Five years pass from the time Paul is arrested in Jerusalem to the end of the book of Acts. In the seven and one-half chapters Luke uses to tell of this experience (about 27 percent of Acts), explicit accounts of power ministries are few and far between in comparison to the other three-fourths of the book. The same is true of evangelism and church planting. This may suggest a relationship between the two, at least for Luke. Although miracles, healings, tongues and prophecies are important ongoing ministries in established churches, for missionaries such as the apostle Paul and for missiology in general, they are much more important on the frontiers of the expansion of the kingdom of God. God uses them to validate the spoken message. Luke previously has stressed this many times by using words such as those describing the ministry of Philip in Samaria as an example: **And the multitudes with one accord heeded the things spoken by Philip, hearing and seeing the miracles which he did (8:6).** Luke also records the report of Paul and Barnabas to the Jerusalem Council by saying: **Then all the multitude kept silent and listened to Barnabas and Paul declaring how many miracles and wonders God had worked through them among the Gentiles (15:12).** Many other examples of such power evangelism can be found.

Now in the final chapter of Acts, although this is not another story of evangelism and church planting, Luke reminds us that the supernatural power of God continues to be manifested by using two vivid anecdotes. Here is the first anecdote:

28:3. But when Paul had gathered a bundle of sticks and laid them on the fire, a viper came out because of the heat, and fastened on his hand.

4. So when the natives saw the creature hanging from his hand, they said to one another, "No doubt this man is a

> murderer, whom, though he has escaped the sea,
> yet justice does not allow to live."
> 5. But he shook off the creature into the fire
> and suffered no harm.
> 6. However, they were expecting that he would swell up
> or suddenly fall down dead. But after they had looked for
> a long time and saw no harm come to him, they changed
> their minds and said that he was a god.

....

Saved from a Snakebite

Although scholarly debates consider whether or not this passage was part of the original Greek, the words of Jesus at the conclusion of the Gospel of Mark relate exactly to Paul's experiences on Malta. According to many ancient manuscripts, Jesus said, "Go into all the world and preach the gospel to every creature....And these signs will follow those who believe:...they will take up serpents; and if they drink anything deadly, it will by no means hurt them; they will lay hands on the sick, and they will recover" (Mark 16:15-18).

The clearest example we find of the fulfillment of these words is Paul's snakebite next to the bonfire. It is interesting to see how some interpret this miraculous event. Although he disagrees with them, Simon Kistemaker reports, "Some scholars think that the reptile was a common grass snake that, although it may strike a man, does not harm him."[4] On this premise, it is difficult to explain the expectations of the Malta natives who undoubtedly were thoroughly familiar with the species. They thought for sure Paul would die. If they recognized it as a miracle, we can hardly do less.

Unfortunately, many modern Christians have absorbed so much of the rationalistic mentality of our Western culture that whenever they confront a situation that can be explained either by a miracle of the grace of God or by scientific cause-and-effect, they seem to prefer the latter. Luke, although he was a physician, obviously tells this story to glorify God through highlighting His power.

A Healing Service in Publius's House

This is the second of Luke's two power ministry anecdotes:

> **28:8.** And it happened that the father of Publius lay sick of a fever and dysentery. Paul went in to him and prayed, and he laid his hands on him and healed him.
> **9.** So when this was done, the rest of those on the island who had diseases also came and were healed.

Publius was the **leading citizen of the island** (v. 7), the political head of Malta at the time. He invited some of the stranded passengers, including at least Luke and Paul, to spend three days at his home, which undoubtedly would have been well appointed. Publius's father happened to be sick with a serious illness, which has since come to be recognized as "Malta fever."

Before Paul laid hands on the man for healing, Luke says Paul prayed. For what would Paul have been praying? He likely would have been asking God if it was His will that Publius's father be healed at that particular time. The words of Jesus come to mind: "Most assuredly, I say to you, the Son can do nothing of Himself, but what He sees the Father do; for whatever He does, the Son also does in like manner" (John 5:19). Before ministering in a situation requiring a miracle, Jesus would have made sure it was His Father's will. Much more, then, Paul needed to do the same. We also recall that when Peter raised Dorcas from the dead, **[he] put them all out, and knelt down and prayed** (Acts 9:40).

Apparently, Paul received a heavenly green light because he then laid on hands on Publius's father, as Jesus had said believers were to do. The man was healed, and not surprisingly the word was spread around the area. It wouldn't have taken long for the people on Malta, which was only 18 miles long and 8 miles wide, to hear the good news about the miracle. Before long, a healing line of sorts apparently had formed outside of Publius's home, and Paul found himself in the midst of a large healing service. From the way Luke tells it, extraordinary healing power must have been present, for all who came apparently were healed.

Although it happened frequently with Jesus, it is rare today to see *all* the sick healed during a healing service. But at times, not all were healed in Jesus' ministry either. For example, Jesus was frustrated with His ministry in His own hometown of Nazareth when He couldn't do many miracles there "because of their unbelief" (Matt. 13:58), and Jesus healed only one out of a great multitude of sick people at the pool of Bethesda (see John 5:1-9). The apostle Paul, who evidently had the gift of healing, had previously failed also. When he later writes a letter to Timothy, he says, "Erastus stayed in Corinth, but Trophimus I have left in Miletus sick" (2 Tim. 4:20). It would be hard to imagine that Paul hadn't prayed for Trophimus's healing, nevertheless, he did not get well.

This time on Malta, however, it was not that way. And the people naturally were most grateful. They showered Paul, Luke and the others with gifts, providing all they needed to continue their journey to Rome in relative comfort. It seems that Paul was not reluctant to receive love offerings in recognition of his healing ministry.

The Last Lap

....

28:11. After three months we sailed in an Alexandrian ship whose figurehead was the Twin Brothers,

which had wintered at the island.
13. ...we came to Puteoli,
14. where we found brethren, and were invited to stay
with them seven days. And so we went toward Rome.

Puteoli was the Italian harbor at which they terminated the grueling sea journey. Rome lay about 120 miles north by land. Apparently, the gospel had been spreading well in Italy, for Puteoli had a church by then and apparently Julius allowed the missionaries to spend a week there. During that time, they had sent word to the believers in Rome that Paul was on his way:

15. And from there, when the brethren heard about us,
they came to meet us as far as Appii Forum and
Three Inns. When Paul saw them, he thanked God
and took courage.

Much to Paul's joy, the believers from many of the Roman house churches had come to meet him on the road and accompany him to Rome.

Settling In at Rome

16. Now when we came to Rome, the centurion
delivered the prisoners to the captain of the guard;
but Paul was permitted to dwell by himself with the
soldier who guarded him.

Staying in his own home gave Paul the freedom to meet with and minister to many people in Rome. He had come because the Jews in Jerusalem had first tried to kill him, then attempted to have him convicted by the Romans of a crime. Neither one had been successful, and now he was to stand trial before Caesar. One thing he naturally would want to know as soon as possible was how he faired with the Jews in Rome. Rome had a large Jewish population, perhaps some 40,000 at the time.

Because Paul could not live in his usual residence in the Jewish quarter and begin attending the synagogue, as was his custom, this time he had to call for the Jewish leaders to come to him:

> **17. And it came to pass after three days that Paul called the leaders of the Jews together....**

He would, undoubtedly, have been greatly relieved by their comment:

> **21. Then they said to him, "We neither received letters from Judea concerning you, nor have any of the brethren who came reported or spoken any evil of you.**
> **22. But we desire to hear from you what you think; for concerning this sect, we know that it is spoken against everywhere."**

Paul's sessions with the Roman Jews turned out the way most of his prior ministry to the Jews had gone. He spoke to them about salvation through faith in Jesus as Messiah, and some believed. But, as usual, communication broke down when the matter of the Gentiles surfaced. Jews in Rome could not handle, any better than other Jews, the fact that God through Jesus Christ had invited Gentiles to share the same salvation, and that they could have it on the basis of faith in Jesus, not by first becoming Jews. They could not imagine that Gentiles could be considered equal to Jews in God's sight.

> 28. "Therefore let it be known to you that the salvation of God has been sent to the Gentiles, and they will hear it!"
> 29. And when he had said these words, the Jews departed and had a great dispute among themselves.

Two Years Preaching the Kingdom of God

> 30. Then Paul dwelt two whole years in his own rented house, and received all who came to him,
> 31. preaching the kingdom of God and teaching the things which concern the Lord Jesus Christ with all confidence, no one forbidding him.

The book of Acts ends where it began—preaching the kingdom of God. Acts begins with Jesus gathered with His disciples, before Paul was a believer, **speaking of the things pertaining to the kingdom of God** (1:3). Thirty years later, the kingdom of God had indeed spread into many parts of the Roman Empire through Peter, John, Stephen, Philip, Barnabas, Paul, Silas, Timothy, Luke and many others whose names we will never know. The fulfillment of Jesus' desire that His followers "make disciples of all the nations" (Matt. 28:19) had started with great power and determination. It has continued through almost 2,000 years, and now for the first time in history some missiologists are saying that there is light at the end of the tunnel. It is not beyond the realm of possibility that the Great Commission can actually be fulfilled in our generation!

To the degree that we use Acts as our missionary training manual, that possibility can more readily become a reality.

Reflection Questions

1. On the ship, the word Paul heard from God could have prevented a disaster. Why is it so hard to make some people believe that God really speaks true things to people today?
2. Do you think our churches would be better off if we made more room for the gift of prophecy? What would this take?
3. A poisonous snake bit Paul, and he didn't die. Some churches today actually handle poisonous snakes in their services to demonstrate the power of God. What do you think of that?
4. For two years, Paul, under arrest, ministered to those who came to visit him. Knowing what we know about Paul, what do you think would have been his major themes?
5. This concludes our study of Acts. In light of what we have seen, name two or three things you think we should be doing in our churches today more than we have been doing.

Notes

1. John Stott, *The Spirit, the Church and the World: The Message of Acts* (Downers Grove, Ill.: InterVarsity Press, 1990), p. 383.
2. William Mitchell Ramsay, *St. Paul the Traveller and the Roman Citizen* (London, England: Hodder & Stoughton, 1925), p. 314.
3. Ibid.
4. Simon J. Kistemaker, *Exposition of the Acts of the Apostles* (Grand Rapids: Baker Book House, 1990), p. 948.

INDEX

More Resources to Move Your Church to Action

Spreading the Fire
C. Peter Wagner
Spreading the Fire takes a penetrating verse-by-verse look at the first eight chapters of Acts, helping readers gain a firm understanding of the Holy Spirit's direction for today's Church.

Book 1 in a three-book series.
Hardcover • ISBN 08307.17102

Lighting the World
C. Peter Wagner
The second book in the Acts of the Holy Spirit Series shows how the Gospel first spread throughout the world—and how it spreads today.

Book 2 in a three-book series.
Hardcover • ISBN 08307.17188

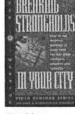

Strategies for Church Growth
C. Peter Wagner
The latest strategies for fulfilling the Great Commission. Program ideas for pastors, missions boards and evangelical coordinators.

Paperback • ISBN 08307.11708

The Prayer Warrior Series

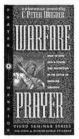

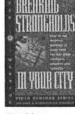

Warfare Prayer
C. Peter Wagner
Here is a biblical and factual guide that will help erase your fears and doubts, leading you to new levels of prayer. Includes questions for individual or group use.
Paperback
ISBN 08307.15134
Video Seminar
SPCN 85116.00612

Prayer Shield
C. Peter Wagner
A powerful tool to help organize and mobilize intercessors in the church. Includes questions for individual or group study.
Paperback
ISBN 08307.15142
Video Seminar
SPCN 85116.00620

Breaking Strongholds in Your City
Edited by C. Peter Wagner
Shows you how to identify the enemy's territory in your city, focus your prayers and take back your neighborhoods for God.
Paperback
ISBN 08307.16386
Video Seminar
SPCN 85116.00647

Churches That Pray
C. Peter Wagner
A comprehensive examination of what prayer is and what it does, how prayer builds the local church and how new forms of prayer can break down the walls between the church and the community—locally and globally.
Paperback
ISBN 08307.16580
Video Seminar
SPCN 85116.00639

Ask for these resources at your local Christian bookstore.

Regal Books
A Division of Gospel Light